Praise for
The Third Screen and Chuck Martin

"Chuck Martin has more than all the facts. He has the soul of the idea. *The Third Screen* is thoughtful and valuable."

> — Chris Brogan, President, Human Business Works and
> co-author of *Trust Agents*

"*The Third Screen* describes a clear power shift where the customer is in charge—and what companies must do their best to reach them on their terms. Using detailed case studies, Chuck Martin shows readers how to develop a mobile marketing strategy that will really work. Don't wait: Get copies for your team today."

> — Charlene Li, bestselling author of
> *Groundswell* and *Open Leadership*

"A fascinating and eye-opening view of the mobile landscape and what companies must do to survive there."

> — Josh Koppel, cofounder ScrollMotion,
> leading mobile platform developer

"Our mobile devices are indispensable digital co-pilots, which is why the third screen is fast becoming the most important screen. If you want to stay relevant to your customers as they go about their lives, apply the lessons from this book."

> —Don Tapscott, author /coauthor of more than 14 books, including the
> bestseller *Wikinomics* and his latest *Macrowikinomics*

"In today's mobile environment, smartphones and tablets have become ubiquitous around the globe. In *The Third Screen*, Chuck Martin engages the reader with important details relating to how the untethered consumer, m-commerce, and the entire mobile revolution are changing the game for marketers and what they need to do to make sure their organizations survive and prosper in this ever-changing and evolving marketplace."

> — Kent Huffman, Chief Marketing Officer at BearCom Wireless and
> Co-Publisher of *Social Media Marketing Magazine*

"Mobile is the ultimate social device. And if big and small brands don't understand how to engage their customers there, they risk extinction. *The Third Screen* is a must-have for any company looking to develop an effective mobile strategy, one that will drive customers to become brand champions."

— Julie Roehm, Marketing Strategy Consultant

"Marketing is ever-changing and *The Third Screen* mirrors the future of marketing. If you are new to mobile, this book makes sure you get it right!"

— Jeffrey Hayzlett, bestselling author of *The Mirror Test*, CMO, Cowboy

"*The Third Screen* distills the opportunities mobile marketing presents to business leaders in an engaging and enjoyable book."

— Jane McPherson, CMO, SpyderLynk, mobile start-up

THE
THIRD
SCREEN

*Marketing to Your Customers
in a World Gone Mobile*

CHUCK MARTIN

NICHOLAS BREALEY
PUBLISHING

BOSTON • LONDON

First published by Nicholas Brealey Publishing in 2011.

20 Park Plaza, Suite 1115A
Boston, MA 02116,
Tel: + 617-523-3801
Fax: + 617-523-3708

3-5 Spafield Street, Clerkenwell
USA London, EC1R 4QB, UK
Tel: +44 (0)20 7239 0360
Fax: +44 (0)20 7239 0370

www.nicholasbrealey.com

© 2011 by Chuck Martin

Printed in the United States of America

15   14   13   12   2   3   4   5

ISBN: 978-1-85788-564-4

Library of Congress Cataloging-in-Publication Data

Martin, Chuck, 1949–
    The third screen : marketing to your customers in a world gone mobile / Chuck Martin.
        p. cm.
    Includes bibliographical references and index.
    ISBN 978-1-85788-564-4
    1. Telemarketing.   2. Mobile commerce.   3. Smartphones.   4. Internet marketing.   5. Internet advertising.   6. Business enterprises—Computer networks.   I. Title.
    HF5415.1265.M3288 2011
    658.8'72—dc22

                                                    2011002406

To Ryan and Chase,
Our sons,
And active members of the mobile revolution

CONTENTS

Contents

Contents

FOREWORD

There is no question about it—the world has changed—it has gone mobile. Your customers are free from the confines of their homes, offices, and traditional media and retail environments. Today, your customers have the power at their fingertips to fulfill their needs anytime and anywhere, and they are using it. They are consuming media (news, radio, television, books, music, advertising) and searching, identifying, locating, and acquiring whatever they need—information, goods and or services—right from the palm of their hand.

Billions of people around the globe are using mobile solutions to enrich and fulfill their lives. They are messaging to get the latest deal, using the camera on their phone to scan product packaging, the mobile browser to find a local store, the mobile Internet to embrace rich media, mobile applications to engage their favorite brands, and voice, location, and mobile commerce services to accomplish so much more. As Chuck Martin points out in *The Third Screen*, the world gone mobile is not a simple story of technological change, it is a story of fundamental shifts in consumer behavior that are forever changing the practice of marketing and how you should view its application with your business.

In order to succeed in today's marketplace, you should not only prepare yourself and your business to be mobile but actually go out there and *be* mobile. Your customers are already mobile and you should be too. To be mobile, you must have a fundamental understanding of your customer and their needs *and* you must also develop a promotional strategy and persistent presence that leverages all that mobile has to offer. If you're not sure who your customer is within the context of mobile, or what it means to be promotional with mobile, or have a persistent presence in mobile, then this book is a must read.

In *The Third Screen* Chuck Martin provides practical and actionable insights from over one thousand executive interviews throughout the mobile industry in order to help you "market to your customers in a world gone mobile". He illustrates the power of mobile through detailed commentary, definitions, and concrete case studies and shows you how mobile, deployed properly, can have a positive impact on your business. In these pages you'll learn the nuances of smartphones, the mobile Web, applications, search, messaging, and most importantly how to engage your *untethered customer* in a real-time, location aware, mobile commerce-enabled context that adheres to industry best practices and regional regulation.

I highly recommend this book. Whether you're new to the concept of mobile and mobile marketing or a veteran in the industry, *The Third Screen* will be a thought provoking and valuable resource for you and your team.

Michael J. Becker
Managing Director, Mobile Marketing Association
Co-author of *Mobile Marketing for Dummies and Web Marketing All-in-One for Dummies*,
Publisher of the *International Journal of Mobile Marketing*

ACKNOWLEDGMENTS

During the many months that we worked on this book, there were numerous people who helped along the way to whom I am very grateful.

I want to say thank you to all those business leaders participating in the mobile revolution who took time from their busy schedules to share their insights and highlight their best practices with me. They were very forthcoming in what they are doing in mobile as well as how they see their course going forward. These include heads of mobile companies, from startups to well-established firms, mobile marketers, and executives leading the mobile efforts inside brands large and small.

Thank you to Erika Heilman, Vice President, Editorial Director of Nicholas Brealey Publishing, North America, for grasping the significance of the mobile revolution and for overall editorial direction in this book. Thank you to Jacquie Flynn, literary agent at Joelle Delbourgo Associates, and still an editor at heart, for recognizing the mobile future early and sharing many discussions on the direction of the book. Thanks to Rusty Shelton of Shelton Interactive for helping arrange activities at SXSW in Austin as part of the book launch.

Thanks to Hayley Comeau and Jill Granucci, Directors of Marketing and Publicity at the Mobile Future Institute, for research and advance marketing of the book, especially to the press and national speakers bureaus, and to Hillary Brodsky at Nicholas Brealey Publishing for advance publicity. Thanks to Justin Elkherj and Zach Tyler,

Directors of Research at Mobile Future Institute, for conducting the mobile surveys, some of which are in this book.

Thanks to Joe Mandese, editor-in-chief of MediaPost who, while briskly walking up a New York City street on our way to a meeting, shared with me the concept of the untethered consumer, a term MediaPost was at that time beginning to use in its marketing materials of its OMMA mobile conferences. This is a term we came to use throughout the book. And thanks to Ken Fadner, Chairman and Publisher of MediaPost, for providing me the opportunity to direct the research efforts at The Center for Media Research at MediaPost Communications, and for being brand manager of the Mobile Insider Summits, where we interact for days at a time with those leading the mobile revolution.

For introductions to executives at major brands, thanks to Hugh Jedwill at the Heartland Mobile Council and to Kent Huffman at *Social Media Marketing Magazine* and Jeff Ashcroft at The Social CMO for providing platforms for sharing the knowledge about mobile.

We want to also acknowledge many on the MediaPost team who work diligently to bring mobile and digital insights to the marketplace through multiple conferences and summits, so credit goes to Rob McEvily, Jeff Loechner, Jon Whitfield, Jonathan McEwan, Sergei Kogut, Elaine Wong, Ross Fadner, Liam Fleming, Seth Oilman, Junmian Sun, Lauren Honig, Steve Smith, and the rest of the team.

Many thanks to the speakers bureaus around the country who represent me and help get the word out. And kudos to all those student-researchers at the Whittemore School of Business and Economics at the University of New Hampshire who diligently conducted two large mobile usage studies examining phone usage among college students.

Most importantly, I want to offer my heartfelt and deepest appreciation to my family without whom this book could not have been written. To Teri, my loving wife and lifelong partner, thank you for all you do, it is a lot. And Ryan and Chase, our sons, to whom this book is dedicated, thank you for your encouragement, patience, and for the sharing of your mobile insights (and indulging in mine).

INTRODUCTION

Mobile Is Game Changing

We're in the midst of a technological revolution bigger than the ones spawned by television or the personal computer, and businesses face a challenging question: how do we, as marketers, harness mobile technology to serve our customers most effectively? The new market is mobile and it's about to change everything.

No longer will the customer be tethered to a television or computer screen, perfectly positioned to receive a message on the marketer's terms. The mobile consumer is on the move, and marketers will have to learn how and where their customers aggregate in this new digital landscape, as well as how to interact with them effectively.

Mobile marketing represents a qualitative change from past marketing methods. The relationship of the consumer to the device is not the passive "lean back" of TV or the more active "lean forward" of the PC, but rather the fully interactive *"pull it forward"* of mobile. It's up close, it's personal, and it's always on.

The first screen, television, revolutionized the way marketers reached consumers, allowing a company to touch millions with well-crafted and tested messages that the company controlled. Families watched the same programming and all were exposed to the same commercial messages.

The first screen allowed one-way communication from one company to many customers. This one-to-many broadcast model allowed companies like Procter & Gamble and General Motors to reach millions of consumers simultaneously with well-developed messages. The marketer was in the driver's seat.

The second screen, the personal computer, fostered interactivity; it allowed companies to communicate with and sell to their customers, easily gaining customer feedback and even permitting customers to provide input on the development of products or services. The model moved from mass marketing to participatory marketing, where consumers could tap into extensive online networks of information about a company's products and services.

These screen revolutions created new consumer behaviors and modified old ones. Catchy television commercials became part of popular culture; customers found themselves singing jingles and recalling memorable and sometimes funny taglines. The advent of Web marketing led consumers to become more interactive, and they got used to communicating more directly with the brands they liked or were considering buying.

The third screen—the smartphone—enables customers to communicate directly with each other more easily and to share information and opinions not only in real time but also as they move from location to location. The challenge and opportunity for businesses is to become part of those conversations and to add value to them.

The third screen revolution has been a long time in the making, and is driven by two significant aspects. One is technological and the other is behavioral, and this book details both and shows how forward-thinking companies are capitalizing on this profound mobile transformation.

The first two revolutions pale when compared with this third screen revolution. Smartphones, in which PC-type capabilities converge with mobile technology, are about to revolutionize the way people behave, interact, consume, and live. Much of the technology for this revolution, in development for years, is now here and is already driving dramatic changes in consumer behavior.

While some mobile technology initially developed in other parts of the world, the playing field has been leveled in recent years. For example, a Toyota subsidiary in the mid 1990s introduced in Japan special codes that are easily read by phones. The next generation of those codes is now in use throughout the United States and Europe. While consumers in South Korea have been able to watch TV on their cell phones for years, consumers in the West now have that capacity as well; it is available on any smartphone with a simple download. And sophisticated smartphones are expanding globally, with Apple's latest iPhone introduced into more than seventeen countries. Brands and marketers are capitalizing on mobile's various forms around the world, ranging from location-based mobile web campaigns in the United Kingdom to mobile reverse auctions in Nigeria to mobile movie promotions in Hong Kong.

This new wave of digital mobility is leading to what we call the *untethered consumer*. Untethered consumers are freed from the constraints of awaiting a broadcast message or any form of traditional online communication from a company. These post-PC consumers are on the move, and are willing and able to use their always-on mobile technology to act and interact with each other and with providers of the products and services they seek out. They are in control, and marketers will be challenged to serve their needs and to interact with them in meaningful ways.

Mobile is a game changer: m-commerce is not just about using the phone to pay for something, it is about revolutionizing the entire buying process, from product research all the way through transaction, based on location. With mobile, marketing can be *hyperlocal*, that is, concerned with a specific, targeted geographic area. Serving the specific needs of users when and where those needs arise is what m-commerce is all about.

Mobile marketing involves much more than providing coupons and discounts. It's about committing to interactions with your customers when and where they choose and defining the future of your brand in the mobile environment.

The Under-the-Radar Revolution

The state of the mobile industry today is similar to the position of the World Wide Web in 1995. The mobile industry is in a mode of rapid growth, and many in the industry view mobile as an explosive business revolution in the making. Hundreds of mobile start-up companies are innovating, scrambling, creating, launching, refocusing, and selling to businesses, many quite successfully. Venture company money is flowing throughout the marketplace, with investors looking for the next mobile version of Google or Facebook.

A significant difference between the Web of the mid-1990s and the current mobile environment is that the network infrastructure of businesses and customers is already in place and everybody is on the Web. Another notable difference is that everyone already has a phone, and most consumers are moving rapidly to smartphones. And the third and perhaps most important difference is that many of the leaders in the mobile industry have a digital, interactive background, having gained experience from the evolution of Web business models. Many of the people working in mobile helped drive in the age of the Internet, and they know what does and doesn't work. They're not experimenting with a digital interactive model, they *know* it. They have been there, done that, and now have the experience to do more right the first time. They understand the business models and revenue sources.

Just as with the advent of Web marketing, there's been a proliferation of mobile companies, many of them start-ups based in cities like New York, Los Angeles, Chicago, London, Austin, Boston, and Montreal; more than a thousand such mobile start-ups have been funded by venture capital firms in the last few years.[1] In many of the offices, everyone is working heads down or on the phone (mobile, of course).

Some of these mobile companies are better known than others. As we visited with many of them and talked to leaders of many of the mobile start-ups, we found several common characteristics:

- All see mobile as a revolutionary force in the marketing industry; they believe that mobile marketing is at a defining point.
- With some notable exceptions, mobile companies find it challenging to get businesses to pursue mobile marketing as significantly as they think the companies should. They are perplexed that some companies don't see it.
- They're not watching competitors as much as they're working to build and fine-tune their own businesses.

- They are intent on creating platforms and new ways of reaching and interacting with mobile customers.

Throughout this book we detail many of the companies taking advantage of emerging mobile markets, exploring what it is they do and how businesses are deploying new mobile technologies. We also profile brands and other businesses that are moving forward with mobile marketing, looking at what they are doing and what they have discovered along the way. Our intent is to show you how much *can* be done by the mobile industry as well as what *is* being done by businesses of all types.

Mobile marketing is surging in a very big way, and that old adage about a rising tide lifting all boats does not hold true for those that are anchored. Those boats sink. The question for businesses is whether they will raise their anchors or remain tethered during the mobile revolution.

Mobile Is Unique

There are unique attributes of the smartphone that require marketers to look carefully at the best ways to interact with untethered consumers. Marketing to mobile users is different from marketing to television audiences or PC users in a number of ways.

It's Personal. The mobile phone is an individual's device. It is not shared like a computer or watched in a group like a television. It is in a person's hand, or pocket, or purse. It is close to her and goes everywhere she goes. After keys and wallet, people make sure they have their phone before leaving home. The communications from the device are personal, including text messages from family and friends, along with social networking connections. To interact through these personal devices, companies need to be invited in, leading to the potential for truly personal marketing.

Multifaceted Communications Capability. The smartphone is the ultimate communications device, and uses almost all the senses in either input or output. A person can communicate by voice, by typing, or by tapping, and he can take, send, and receive pictures and videos, as well as read, record voice, or scan.

Time, Location, and Supply and Demand. While supply and demand always have been determinable, never before could time and location be added to the mix. Mobile allows that. With location-based technology built into smartphones, marketers can determine precise customer location and, coupled with time, create highly targeted and relevant marketing messages based on that time and location in relation to their products and services. They can use previous location research to create new value to the customer. Location awareness alone changes everything.

The Standing Up Medium. Mobile removes all the content consumption constraints of previous media. Movies, TV, radio, and even Web content are consumed mostly while stationary and while sitting. A person *could* watch a movie or TV while standing up, but it is not the *best* way to use the media. Sound is somewhat different, as a person can listen to an MP3 player while on the go, but there is still the limited interaction of simply changing song or station. Mobile is a standing-up content consumption medium. You *can*, of course, use mobile while sitting still, but it is more likely you will use it while standing and often while, well, mobile. While waiting for a bus or train, the untethered consumer can do a quick e-mail check. He can read a communication from the office and send a reply while in line at the airport. Mobile is the ultimate digital communications medium while in transit. Businesspeople often check e-mail or text messages while in meetings or attending conferences. Students may check for messages between classes (or some, under the desk during class). Untethered consumers constantly share information with each other, wherever they are.

Installed Base. There has never been as large an installed base of technological products as mobile phones. Market penetration is nearing 100 percent in many countries; in the United States, nine out of ten people have a phone. And that market is always live. The sheer numbers of people with mobile phones provides opportunity to reach substantial markets through the massive medium of mobile.

Ramp-Up Speed. When the Web began to grow, everyone had to start from scratch to get connected. There were no businesses or consumers online and connected to each other; each one had to start from the beginning. With mobile, the network is already in place, as people and businesses are connected to the Internet through computers and other devices. Mobile easily taps into that network, as well as the network of knowledge of the digital, interactive business place.

Self-Service Platforms. Many mobile companies built self-service platforms for businesses to use, setting them up this way because Web infrastructure and technical capabilities were already in place. Many in the mobile industry have created self-service tools for marketers to use (you'll see many examples of this throughout the book), allowing them to more quickly and efficiently interact with mobile customers as well as track those interactions in great detail. Many mobile companies focus on enabling marketers to take advantage of mobile rather than doing mobile marketing for them.

Call-to-Action Capability. The customer has the phone, it is on, and the mindset of the customer can be well determined based on factors including time and location. Because of these capabilities and the intimate nature of the device, companies can issue an on-the-spot call to action for the customer. This could range from a "buy now" offer prompted by a customer on location in a competitor's store to a discount offer for an additional product based on the item being ordered via mobile. These calls to action can be included in text or video messages, or via mobile website or branded applications.

The Mobile Ecosystem. There is an entire ecosystem built around mobile that includes the cell phone carriers, device makers, a multitude of mobile platforms of all types and categories, and hundreds of thousands of smartphone applications. It is the breadth of this system that comprises the underlying platform of mobile. More and more companies are plugging into this complex ecosystem.

Customer-Centric. In a world gone mobile, the customer is in the
driver's seat. Everything starts with untethered consumers, since
they start with their phone. Customers can base their starting
action according to their current location, since their phone will
tell these customers where they are in context of all around them,
such as proximity to a particular store or product.

The Mobile Market

Five billion people in the world have cell phones. That's 73 percent
of the entire population of the world.[2] The dramatic growth in the
number of cell phones around the world can hardly be overstated. For
context, there are roughly a billion personal computers and two billion
televisions worldwide. During the past five years, the number of cell
phones in use around the world has doubled,[3] and projections are for
continued growth.

In the United States, the percentages are even higher, with more
than 297 million people owning cell phones—94 percent of the total
population.[4] And while more and more people were latching on to cell
phones, many were simultaneously dropping their landlines. Within a
five-year period, twenty-three million people in the United States cut
the cord.[5] In the same period globally, there were fifty-seven million
fewer fixed telephone lines but 1.9 billion additional mobile cellular
subscriptions.[6] No matter how you look at it, the growth of mobile has
been astounding; it is the most quickly adopted technology in history,
surpassing even Internet use every step of the way.

Mobile adoption is being driven by technological advances, including higher connection speeds, more widely available Internet access,
and a flood of applications that provide almost any mobile feature
imaginable. And this is not a U.S.-only phenomenon. Other countries
have been leading the way in several areas, including mobile transactions, and growth everywhere is clear.

- Nine out of ten mobile users in China text on their phones.[7] In
  Japan, consumers swipe cell phones rather than credit cards for

payment, and in South Korea, free mobile television has been around for five years. Broadcasters there say almost thirty million people watch TV regularly from their phones.

- Four out of five people in the United States have mobile phones, and at least half of them will own smartphones by the end of 2011. This phenomenon is creating an increasing ability for everybody to connect with everybody else.
- Many smartphone owners are willing to view ads on mobile devices, leaving marketers who do not adapt at a sizable disadvantage.
- Untethered consumers with smartphones text more, use the Internet more, play more games, use more applications, and listen to music and watch video more than those without smartphones.

Mobile customers are doing a lot more than talking on their phones. They're checking the weather, sending and receiving photos, checking e-mail, watching videos, sending and receiving text messages, researching and purchasing products, reading restaurant reviews, scanning bar codes in stores, downloading coupons, reading, playing games, checking in to locations, finding directions, checking traffic, following sports, social networking, buying movie tickets, listening to the radio, and more. And as more people do more with their phones, they tend to do less talking.[8] Since 1996, the average length of local cell phone calls progressively decreased from a little more than three minutes to less than two minutes.

These mobile activity indicators are barely the tip of the iceberg of mobile's impact on the marketing landscape. More than thirteen million people accessed bank accounts through mobile websites in one month and more than five million people are using banking apps.[9] And that's just one industry. Research we conducted at the Center for Media Research at MediaPost Communications shows that, for the first time, more than half of media spending will be on nontraditional media, and a large percentage of media planners will be moving to mobile. But some of these planners lack an understanding of mobile marketing and worry about how to interact effectively with the untethered consumer. We also found that 41 percent of those not yet doing mobile campaigns did not plan to in the foreseeable future. While many of the large brands are experimenting with mobile, others are taking a wait-and see-approach.

The Untethered Consumer

The move to a world gone mobile is not just about technology; it is about behavioral change. It is subtle and gradual but undeniable. This transformation will be much like the one that Walmart, and later some supermarkets, accomplished when the company "trained" customers to take the bags of merchandise they had just purchased and place them in the carts themselves. There were no directions on how to do it, and many people don't even recall that employees used to load bags into the carts for them. The same is true for supermarket self-checkout and airline self–check-in.

If we told people a decade ago that they would be typing messages with their thumbs, they would not have believed it. Yet today, this is common not only with multitasking teens but with busy business-people using BlackBerry smartphones, iPhones, and Droids. People are reading books on iPhones. Mobile marketers will further change consumer behaviors by facilitating shopping and purchasing directly from mobile phones, often on location.

Throughout this book we will show how these behavioral changes are taking hold, driven by new services and capabilities being deployed by mobile marketing companies. Technology without behavioral change would be relatively meaningless, and marketers and businesspeople who don't understand the implications of the untethered consumer risk obsolescence.

Marketers and advertisers need to reach out to untethered consumers and become part of the conversations as their potential customers communicate with each other through their social networks. It's been shown that consumers are more likely to take a friend's recommendation over a company's, so the potential for group movement to any given product or service is high. Marketing will have to adapt to interact with the untethered consumer. In this environment, the unique selling proposition (USP) becomes Using Smartphone Technology (USPT).

The Mobile End Game

There are several fundamental characteristics of the mobile landscape that offer companies new opportunities to leverage. These characteristics provide marketers with different ways to interact with their customers. These can range from dealing with customers in certain locations at certain times to monitoring how their mobile customers are influencing each other.

Brick-and-Mortar Advantage. The third screen will forever transform the concept of one-to-one marketing, in terms of how a company talks to its customers. Mobile allows companies to communicate directly with the untethered consumer as he shops. This development provides great opportunity for traditional brick-and-mortar retailers, as customers in their stores access real-time information about their products on site; with consumers always accessible via their phones, retailers can capitalize by offering special deals on the spot. Brands of all sizes have been anxiously awaiting this development, which will provide them with the opportunity to conduct what we call *momentary marketing*. Businesses will have the ability to price-match competitors via mobile offers while they have the customer on the premises. Those that miss this opportunity will be severely disadvantaged.

Platforms Win. Among the main drivers of a world gone mobile are the technology platforms on which businesses and untethered consumers ride. Platforms are widely accessible by mobile phone so that consumers can easily tap in and access any relevant or desired content or information at any time. These mobile platforms come in a variety of categories: there are online video platforms, mobile social media platforms, text message platforms, video message platforms, and many more. We'll look at examples of all of these platforms in this book. In mobile, platforms win. They facilitate marketing and transactions, and allow many businesses and customers to join in and participate. This is different from buying a product or service. It is more like riding on the platform. In mobile, platforms rule.

Less Is More. In a world gone mobile, less is more. Businesses need to "Think Small." Thinking small is not about small ideas but about quick, focused delivery. Because of its size, the third screen cannot display as much content as a web page, at least not all at one time. The other driver of the less-is-more philosophy is the reality that people tend to consume mobile content in short bites while on the go. It is easier to consume a little at a time, since mobile phone use is more of a continuous cycle than an event, such as watching a movie. On the phone, it's more practical to view a short video clip.

The Mobile Chicken and Egg. Mobile will drive mobile. As more consumers find new capabilities of their smartphones, they will show these features to others. As more features are discovered, more will be created. The creation of more features—ranging from discounts that can be scanned to applications that make daily life easier—will lead to more adoption by more people. As more people get smartphones, more features will be used, driving the creation of yet more features. This is the *mobile chicken and egg.*

The time for marketers to get into mobile is now. It is a matter of being positioned on the wave or under it. With the mobile revolution there are two types of people: those who see it and those who don't, or, perhaps more accurately, those who believe that mobile is a game changer (it is) and those who do not.

Our intent with this book is to help businesses and marketers better understand the magnitude of this mobile revolution and to detail the ways that savvy companies are effectively deploying mobile marketing with their customers. We hope to demystify the underlying mobile technological issues marketers face, as well as highlight differences between traditional and mobile marketing, some of which are significant. We'll profile many of the models used by businesses that are driving the mobile industry in addition to exploring business leaders' views of the mobile marketplace and how mobile is working for them.

Welcome to the third screen revolution.

The Rise of the Untethered Consumer

Mobile consumers are freed from a desktop computer for access to information or their networks. With total digital mobility, they are always connected and can do virtually anything with anyone, anytime, anywhere. Empowered by the third screen, these are the *untethered consumers*, and they have computing power in their hands wherever they go.

The untethered consumer constantly consumes content from her smartphone, no matter where she is. She watches movie clips while waiting for a bus, checks e-mail on the sidelines of her child's soccer game, reads parts of a book or magazine in spurts throughout the day, and downloads an app she just heard about via a text message from a friend. The untethered consumer has limitless boundaries and can interact wherever she is on her own timeframe. In a world gone mobile, everything is connected to everything and is accessible from anywhere.

Untethered consumers rely on their peers for recommendations, and they trust the recommendations of others more than the promotional messages from the companies that make or market the products. This system of user opinions goes beyond social networking, as consumers reach out to networks of others who may have purchased a particular item, heard certain music, or seen specific movies.

When an untethered consumer loves or hates something, he will let others know in real time. These consumers instantly determine from others the collective view of products and services. And after receiving these recommendations from others, purchasing via the third screen will become commonplace in the United States, as it already has in some countries.

Mobile Is Personal

No two people are alike, and the same is true for smartphones. Think about it: each phone is highly personal and intimate to its owner. Each is personalized, with contact lists, desired applications, and a unique arrangement of applications on the screen. People select their own phone screensaver, and can choose to see a loved one or a favorite vacation spot every time they look at the screen. Each smartphone has a different and personally selected set of applications, placed on the screen where that untethered consumer likes them.

The untethered consumer rarely shares his phone. If he does loan it temporarily and the borrower makes the smallest of changes, the owner recognizes it right away and may even become rattled by the change. Mobile phone platforms add to this individualization. The starting point for each smartphone owner is that phone model's particular universe. Owners of BlackBerry smartphones become familiar with App World and the types of applications available there. They learn how their phone works, how their cell phone carrier operates, and get used to the daily interaction via that phone. Owners of iPhones have their own universe as well, as do owners of phones running Google's Android operating system and owners of Microsoft's Windows Phone 7.

Individuals also settle into their mobile routines, perhaps checking the weather via a mobile app, searching the Web, reading a book, shopping, finding deals, watching videos, and so on. Each person lives in his own personal mobile universe, and each mobile universe is unique.

One of the new dynamics presented by a world gone mobile is a change in perspective. Because the smartphone is so personal and individual, each user tends to view the market from his personal mobile perspective. Marketers seeking larger mobile budgets should be aware of this shift from mass-experienced to personally experienced marketing, because those controlling the budgets may view proposed mobile strategies through their own personal mobile lens, based on the way they use their own phones. Their perspective on what consumers may or may not do with their mobile phones in the future may be limited (or exaggerated) by what they do with their own phones.

The m-Powered Customer

In a world gone mobile, the individual customer has more control than ever before. The mobile customer can check prices on location, compare items against competitors' offerings, and get on-the-spot recommendations from friends and peers. She can find anything directly from her mobile device and connect with others instantly by various means. We call this totally enabled, roving, mobile-empowered customer the m-powered consumer. She is untethered and totally empowered by mobile.

This m-powered customer also can be reached at certain times in specific locations. Never before could both of these pieces of information be factored into marketing, and it opens the door for marketers to customize their campaigns accordingly.

Mobile Makes It Direct

For today's untethered consumer, mobile makes engagement with consumers personal and, because of its personal nature, brings a relevance that no other medium has. Mobile makes the experience of interacting with marketers more personal for the consumer. The device is up close, always on, and can be tailored to individual needs. With mobile, consumers now can easily get information and engage in a range of unique experiences and connect with almost anybody. "Historically, carriers had nearly complete control over the experience consumers would have with their mobile device," says Michael Becker, North American Managing Director of the Mobile Marketing Association.[10] "However, in recent years, as mobile devices have become smarter and more open, this control has diminished." Becker continues: "While carriers still play an invaluable role in enabling our ability to engage through and with mobile, due to the increasing opening of the mobile device, consumers are getting more and more choice in the ability to have a direct relationship with brands." They do, in fact, opt in and willingly agree to receive marketing and other messages from companies sent directly to their phones."

Mobile has become the untethered consumer's primary communication tool, and he uses it not only with friends and family but also with the businesses he interacts with. Consumers interact directly with other consumers through all the available mobile media paths; they also use these paths to engage with brands they trust, and they have proven that they will opt in and agree to receive marketer-initiated communications such as text messages. Moreover, these m-powered consumers use their mobile phones to initiate communication, reaching out to brands and to other consumers with messages and interactions.

This idea of consumers and companies communicating on a one-to-one basis has been the long-sought promise of marketing. Because of the personal nature of a phone, the relationship between the untethered consumer and a company can be essentially closer. No longer is a marketing message sent to the masses, as are traditional television broadcasts. With mobile, the message can be, and indeed must be, more intimate.

"The fundamental change in marketing is that it is becoming increasingly more technological and direct, due to mobile," says Becker. "We all become direct marketers. We are marketing to an individual, and that changes everything." This raises interesting issues, as the customer has to opt in, essentially agreeing to receive marketing information in advance. The untethered consumer can decide to opt in to many businesses, services, or messages or to only a few, depending on a range of factors, from value provided to incentives to participate.

In an industry that is expanding and changing as rapidly as mobile, an organization designed to educate industry players and to investigate and recommend best practices is a valuable enterprise. The Mobile Marketing Association is an industry-leading trade association comprising organizations throughout the entire mobile marketing ecosystem, including advertisers, brands, content owners, mobile carriers, retailers, application providers, and a wide range of other industry players. Its mission is to help promote, educate, measure, guide, and protect the industry. To this end, the association offers educational curricula, has established the industry's most widely adopted best practices, provides research and thought leadership, and helps establish meaningful relationships among all parties within the mobile ecosystem.

The Customer as Mobile Platform

Companies of all types and sizes in every industry and market will be affected by the mobile revolution and the movements of the untethered consumer. The mobile customer becomes a constantly moving target, transitioning near and away from products and services all the time.

The critical factor in serving the untethered consumer is the unique value provided to that customer. These new consumers need a reason to interact with a company; businesses must develop compelling, personalized messages rather than relying on sales pitches designed for broadcast to the masses. Some companies will get this, and some won't. Or, perhaps more accurately, some will get it sooner than others. Those that don't get it won't last long.

As in traditional marketing, one of the most important ingredients of a successful mobile strategy will be satisfying customers with their shopping experience. Companies that have been successful designing superior customer experiences are well positioned to add mobile marketing to their repertoires. Starbucks, for example, provides mobile information about, and photos of, all its coffees and foods, with store locators and maps based on the consumer's current location. As in the brick-and-mortar Starbucks stores, the mobile "store" allows users to customize their drinks as well as those of a friend and save them for later use, e-mail them, or post them to a social network such as Facebook or Twitter. The mobile approach has the same feel as the in-store approach; the company is simply providing value through a different mechanism, while fully utilizing the features of that mechanism.

Like Starbucks, online shoe store Zappos, well known for its legendary and fanatical focus on customer service at all levels, looks at mobile as yet another way to deliver what the company calls "WOW" customer service. "For us, we have selections that most physical stores don't have," says Thomas Knoll, Community Architect at Zappos.[11] "We want to be there and be a service for a customer," says Knoll. "Mobile is the ultimate be-of-service channel for whatever you desire. Loyalty implies a relationship. In mobile, the people I trust the most are the people I know and people like me. The platform we want to have an app on is the person. For mobile, we have to look at each platform and see what each does well."

Mobile is not simply another advertising or marketing channel: it is a new and personal way to interact with your customers and provide increased value to them.

Mobile Drives Behavioral Change

More than 70 percent of executives and managers already use their phones for sending and receiving e-mail and more than half are texting, according to research we conducted at The Mobile Future Institute. Already, forty-five million mobile subscribers regularly use the mobile Internet, and that number has been growing at a rate of 25 percent for each of the past three years.

Don't make the mistake of thinking that this wave is youth-focused either, because the bulk of mobile Internet use comes from adults. While almost 90 percent of eighteen- to twenty-one-year-olds have cell phones, only slightly more than a third (35 percent) have smartphones.[12] Two university-wide studies conducted at the University of New Hampshire in late 2010 also found that slightly more than a third (36 percent) of students owned smartphones. The risk for businesses that do not adapt to the mobile trend is twofold: first, the company will miss opportunities to market and relate to these untethered consumers; second, it will lose customers who find and interact with a competitor instead.

Untethered consumers are doing more on their mobile phones than ever before and plan to do even more over time. They plan to take and send more pictures with their camera phones, use mobile applications, send and receive e-mail, and use the mobile web.[13] But mobile is causing many other changes in behavior. For example:[14]

- Twenty percent of eighteen- to thirty-four-year-olds have brought up a Web page on their phone to show someone a picture or image to enhance their story.

- Almost half of those aged eighteen to thirty-four years have kept someone's number in their phones just so they know not to answer when the person calls.
- More than half of those eighteen- to twenty-four-year-olds have started playing with their mobile phone because another person was or other people were.

These examples are just a small sampling of how behaviors and habits are changing because of mobile phones. People now use cell phones nearly everywhere, which offers marketers a host of new challenges as well as opportunities. For example, 82 percent of mobile phone owners have used their phone in a store, more than half have used it in a doctor's office or hospital, and more than a third at sporting events.[15]

The opportunities to reach these untethered consumers are varied, as long as the marketer can provide true value, such as useful information while the customer shops or fun facts while the user takes in a sporting event. This approach goes beyond traditional advertising; it means marketers have to become highly useful to their customers more often and in more varied locations than ever before.

Another behavioral change in mobile is peer-to-peer information exchange. For example, more than a third of mobile phone users have shopped in stores while on the phone and have asked the person they were talking to about a product. This is a classic case of brand disintermediation, where the brand or the marketer is left out of the discussion; one person potentially persuades a friend to buy, or dissuades him from buying, a product or service. Worse for the marketer, this product discussion is essentially invisible.

This type of shopping behavior will forever change the company–customer interaction. Here, from noted research firm InsightExpress, are the actions mobile users performed while in stores, in order of largest number of people:

- Used mobile phone to take a picture of an item to send to someone
- Used phone to search for item reviews

- Used phone to search for better prices on an item
- Looked for a coupon on their mobile phone
- Used a coupon already on their phone
- Used phone to find a recipe
- Made a purchase using the mobile phone
- Used the phone to compare nutritional information on products
- Scanned a bar code with a mobile phone

The m-powered consumer is not only using the Web on location as they shop, they also are turning to applications while they shop. About 40 percent of those with smartphones with apps say they at least sometimes use apps to make decisions while shopping.[16] And owners of Apple iPhones are even more active, with more than half of them using apps to make shopping decisions. The most common category of products these untethered consumers are using with apps are technology and electronics, about three times more than those using the apps to shop for clothing or groceries.

The untethered consumer will provide marketers with a wealth of new information about how and when they shop and buy, also based on various demographics. For instance, research from InsightExpress shows that the majority of male mobile shoppers who own smartphones, compared to about a quarter of the general population, are more inclined to go searching for coupons.[17] They are m-powered. While almost 40 percent want to receive the coupons at the store via text message, only about a quarter of the general population has the same view.

These are just small indicators of the multitude of behavioral changes that will cause marketing strategies and tactics to evolve to serve the untethered consumer.

Traveling with the Buyers

Cars.com was founded in 1997 as a joint venture of various newspaper companies, as a hedge against the movement of newspaper classified advertising to the Internet. The Times Mirror Company, Tribune Company, and The Washington Post Company together created a company called Classified Ventures, which they based in Chicago. The papers wanted to create one national brand focused on cars. Several months after launch, Knight Ridder, Inc., Central Newspapers, Gannett Co., Inc. (publisher of *USA Today*), and The McClatchy Company joined the venture.[18] These media properties promoted Cars.com through their various print and broadcast outlets.

Within a year of its launch, Cars.com was attracting half a million people a month to its website, where visitors could search online classified ads for cars. Consumers looking to buy a car visit the Cars.com website and enter the make and model they're looking for, their price range, and the search distance from their current zip code. Within seconds, all the cars meeting the criteria are listed, together with dealer or seller information, including phone number and e-mail address. The company successfully created quick, one-stop, online car shopping.

A few years later, the well-known car industry authority Kelley Blue Book partnered with Cars.com, becoming the exclusive provider of used-vehicle information for the online service. In 2004 Cars.com launched a national television campaign and several years later it was advertising during the Super Bowl.

Over the years, Cars.com evolved to provide comprehensive pricing information, photos, buying guides, comparison tools, editorial content, and expert car reviews and related information that helped a car shopper make a decision. Consumers can also place an ad to sell their car online via Cars.com. For car dealers, Cars.com carried advertising, including banner ads and lead generation tools, with the objective of connecting car shoppers with car sellers.

More than ten million car shoppers a month now visit Cars.com, which carries listings of more than two million cars for sale. Benefiting from its origin in newspaper companies, Cars.com partnered with more than 175 local newspaper affiliates and television stations, including their websites, as well as with national websites such as USAToday.com and Yahoo! Autos. It was logical, as well as ironic, that Cars.com should go mobile.

The obvious starting point was to create a mobile version of the Cars.com website so that consumers could search new and used car listings, find dealers and locate them on a map, calculate loan payments, read reviews, and more, all from their phones.

Responsibility for the mobile development and deployment initially came under the Consumer Products Group at Cars.com, and there were different considerations than were necessary for the website. "With the wired Cars.com, there are core listings from dealers, consumer reviews, auto industry information, and more," says Nick Fotis, Products Manager, Mobile, at Cars.com.[19] "With the mobile site, the assumption is that the user is not looking for detailed specs but for cars that are near them now."

The company started with a mobile device–agnostic approach so that the service would work on almost any phone with Internet access. Fotis got involved in the mobile aspects of Cars.com in 2009, after having spent half a dozen years at Cars.com as part of the Consumer Products Group. "I thought it would be big," he says. After the mobile site launch, the company decided to try its hand at launching an app. "We were bullish on doing an iPhone app and business was good so we had the opportunity to do it," says Fotis. "Our decision was less from a technical point of view and more from a distribution point of view. Our premise was that if I have a smartphone there are two options to resolve an information need—both app and browser. We chose Apple because of the activity within the Apple store. Within two months of the iPhone app launch, we had 20 percent more traffic there than on the mobile site."

One of the main differences between mobile interactions on the Cars.com website compared with the iPhone app was speed, as some of the necessary car information was stored in the app, making it dramatically faster than downloading page after page from the mobile website. The app contained less editorial content and also provided the ability to link to the Cars.com website.

"There was not a tremendous amount of cannibalization from the iPhone app," says Fotis. "Search is a lot faster with the app, since with website, the browser has to grab all the information from the web page, while in the app some of the information is already there. But there are still some people who prefer to find information by browser."

This is another example of the behavioral change that some customers will be slower to accept. Even though the Cars.com app is faster, searching websites with browsers has been ingrained in computer users for many years. Part of the adoption cycle occurs by word of mouth, as one customer sees another doing essentially the same thing using an app and noting that the results are better with the app. Another part of the adoption cycle involves learning about a new way of doing things. Not everyone will adopt new technologies and approaches at the same time. Phasing in of users is just part of the learning process that marketers need to be cognizant of while moving to mobile.

However, adoption and success in mobile marketing can and should be measured, and Cars.com carefully tracked the progress of its mobile efforts. Fotis found that users of the Cars.com mobile website viewed an average of twelve to fifteen pages per visit, while users of the iPhone app viewed twenty-five to thirty-five pages per visit. This means an active car shopper using the app can find more options faster, due to the speed of the app.

As consumers use mobile phones to find information earlier in the car shopping process, a lower percentage of people are using phones on the lot, though the total number of people using mobile technologies to shop for cars is higher. "A survey we did in 2008 showed that about 40 percent of participants were using phones on the lot," says Fotis. "Mobile will grow to be replacements for laptops. We're seeing more searching on mobile earlier in the process." Says Fotis:

> Inventory is our core product. Inventory search starts with a person entering a zip code. Our revenue is 80 percent from local dealers and 20 percent from display advertising from manufacturers. Of the 80 percent, a majority is from our core subscription package but we also offer features such as video and credit applications. We currently have no mechanism yet to get that on our mobile site so this is a concern of ours. We've only sold mobile to our national advertisers. It's a lot of data work. The drawback of being first to market is that you have to make sacrifices. We don't yet have the back-end mechanisms to push certain content to mobile products, including video.
>
> We recognized that mobile would be important so we did an iPhone app and saw a 100 percent increase in mobile traffic. It went from 5 percent of our total traffic to 12 percent in two months.

Our core business is linking buyers and sellers, which is inherently a mobile business, so anything we can do to deliver information helps. Mobile is bigger and moving faster that we thought.

The two biggest impacts we see are at the top end, the researching activities of what kinds of cars a person is looking for, and the bottom end on the lot with consumers using negotiation tools.

Fotis learned several lessons along the way, as the company moved to mobile and modified strategy and tactics during the process. "After the launch of the mobile app, I didn't anticipate how many people within the organization have an opinion of what we're doing in mobile," he says. Philosophically, the organization did not look at mobile as an add-on but rather as integral to the entire business. "We're not building a mobile department, we're getting everyone involved. We need to have everyone in the organization aware of and knowledgeable about mobile. We expect 20 to 30 percent of our traffic to be mobile very shortly."

To jump-start its move to mobile, Cars.com hired outside suppliers for various components. The company eventually decided to bring some of the mobile functions and operations in-house. "The level of face-to-face interaction is critical for apps development," says Fotis, who contracted with an out-of-state firm to start some of the mobile operations. "It's not sustainable to use those from the outside, so we're working with a local firm to do an Android app. Organizations also need to determine the overall internal temperature for risk in doing mobile."

Going mobile for Cars.com also meant more than just serving car shoppers. The company wants to empower its sixteen thousand car dealers to add their inventory to the Cars.com mobile website. "We want to let dealers do it on mobile on their lot," says Fotis.

Companies often find that they start with one mobile-related initiative, and that leads to extensions of the initiative. This is partly because mobile devices are being used by people at every stage of the value chain. This includes not only end customers but also salespeople, suppliers, distributors, vendors, business partners, employees, managers, and others. It's only logical that the untethered mobile users at each level of an organization want to be involved with the shift to mobile.

"We have five hundred people selling our products to dealers," says Fotis. "With mobile, they could log their conversations and gather dealer information." Fotis also found unexpected uses of the iPhone app. "It was adopted by the dealers as a competitive research tool, which we didn't think of. The dealers would say 'I'm two swipes away from seeing the cars of my competitors.' There is always a phone present."

Fotis has a goal of gaining better control over mobile products so the company can more easily support them. Cars.com also plans to continue adding mobile platforms and features, such as search notification, which would notify customers when a specific vehicle they are looking for becomes available. "Don't ignore the other platforms," he says. "It's less about the technology and more about the market size."

Long term, Cars.com expects its' business to be split into thirds: a third will come from mobile; a third from tablets, TVs, and apps; and a third from traditional desktop computers. While the Super Bowl ad in 2010 that featured Cars.com mobile caused a 30 percent spike in traffic, it also sees as large and even larger increases during the holiday season. The other large spikes in traffic that occur daily, with people sitting at their desks during lunchtime, are now coming more and more from mobile phones.

Global Mobile

Make no mistake, the untethered consumer is everywhere on the planet. Whether your company's marketing strategy involves global branding or local tactics to support a specific product launch, the untethered consumer will be a factor in the success of your marketing campaigns. Cell phone market penetration is growing, and the number of cell phones already exceeds the entire population in seventy-five countries around the world (see Table 1).

Mobile is global, with brands expanding to use mobile marketing in various ways in all types of markets. For example, sportswear maker Puma launched a mobile initiative in thirteen world markets for soccer enthusiasts. The company used mobile to connect friends and fans of the same soccer team. Users downloaded their team's song so that when their team scored they were instantly alerted and (for free) teleconferenced in

TABLE 1: 75 COUNTRIES WHERE CELL PHONE PENETRATION EXCEEDS POPULATION[20]

Country	Mobile Penetration	Population	Mobile Subscribers
United Arab Emirates	232%	4,600,000	10,671,900
Estonia	203%	1,340,000	2,720,500
Bahrain	200%	790,000	1,578,000
Macao, China	192%	540,000	1,037,400
Qatar	175%	1,410,000	2,472,100
Saudi Arabia	174%	25,720,000	44,864,400
Hong Kong, China	174%	7,020,000	12,206,900
St. Kitts and Nevis	166%	50,000	83,000
Panama	165%	3,450,000	5,677,100
Russia	164%	140,870,000	230,500,000
Dominica	151%	70,000	106,000
Italy	151%	59,870,000	90,613,000
Lithuania	151%	3,290,000	4,961,500
Antigua & Barbuda	150%	90,000	134,900
Maldives	148%	310,000	457,800
Trinidad & Tobago	147%	1,340,000	1,970,000
Suriname	147%	520,000	763,900
Luxembourg	147%	490,000	719,000
Finland	144%	5,330,000	7,700,000
Portugal	142%	10,710,000	15,178,000
Bermuda	142%	60,000	85,000
Austria	141%	8,360,000	11,773,000
Bulgaria	141%	7,540,000	10,617,100
Singapore	140%	4,740,000	6,652,000
Oman	139%	2,850,000	3,970,600
Czech Republic	138%	10,370,000	14,258,400
Croatia	137%	4,420,000	6,035,100
Denmark	135%	5,470,000	7,406,000
Anguilla	135%	20,000	27,000
Albania	132%	3,160,000	4,161,600
United Kingdom	131%	61,570,000	80,375,400
Barbados	130%	260,000	337,100
Argentina	129%	40,280,000	51,891,000
Germany	128%	82,170,000	105,000,000

TABLE 1: 75 COUNTRIES WHERE CELL PHONE PENETRATION EXCEEDS POPULATION[20] (Cont.)

Country	Mobile Penetration	Population	Mobile Subscribers
Netherlands	128%	16,590,000	21,182,000
Israel	126%	7,170,000	9,022,000
Sweden	124%	9,250,000	11,426,000
Guatemala	123%	14,030,000	17,307,500
El Salvador	123%	6,160,000	7,566,200
Thailand	123%	67,760,000	83,057,000
Switzerland	122%	7,570,000	9,255,000
Montenegro	121%	620,000	752,000
Ukraine	121%	45,710,000	55,333,200
British Virgin Islands	120%	20,000	24,000
Romania	119%	21,270,000	25,377,000
Greece	119%	11,160,000	13,295,100
Hungary	118%	9,990,000	11,792,500
Poland	117%	38,070,000	44,553,100
Taiwan, Province of China	117%	23,100,000	26,958,800
Belgium	117%	10,650,000	12,419,000
Aruba	116%	110,000	128,000
Seychelles	115%	80,000	92,300
Faroe Islands	114%	50,000	57,000
Australia	114%	21,290,000	24,220,000
Spain	114%	44,900,000	50,991,100
Uruguay	113%	3,360,000	3,802,000
Cyprus	112%	870,000	977,500
Norway	111%	4,810,000	5,336,000
Malaysia	111%	27,470,000	30,379,000
St. Vincent and the Grenadines	110%	110,000	121,100
New Zealand	110%	4,270,000	4,700,000
Jamaica	109%	2,720,000	2,971,300
Iceland	109%	320,000	349,000
Ireland	108%	4,520,000	4,871,100
Brunei Darussalam	107%	400,000	426,300
Bahamas	106%	340,000	358,800
Slovenia	104%	2,020,000	2,100,400
St. Lucia	104%	170,000	176,000

TABLE 1: 75 COUNTRIES WHERE CELL PHONE PENETRATION EXCEEDS POPULATION[20] (Cont.)

Country	Mobile Penetration	Population	Mobile Subscribers
Honduras	103%	7,470,000	7,714,000
Malta	103%	410,000	422,100
Slovak Republic	102%	5,410,000	5,497,700
Serbia	101%	9,850,000	9,912,300
Belarus	101%	9,630,000	9,686,200
Viet Nam	101%	88,070,000	88,566,000
Ecuador	100%	13,630,000	13,634,800

with their chosen friends or a network of anonymous supporters. Following are a few examples of ways mobile marketing is being deployed in various countries.

China. With more than 750 million cell phone subscribers, half the population of China has a cell phone, making it the world's largest mobile device market.[21] Almost 40 percent of those subscribers access the Web by phone, compared to about 25 percent in the United States. In China, a larger percentage of users are texting than in the United States, but a much larger percentage of phone users in the United States use their phones for e-mail.

> **Top uses of mobile phones in China:**[22]
> Text messaging, SMS—87%
> Games—39%
> Mobile Internet—37%
> Ringtone downloads—26%
> Instant messaging—23%
> Picture messaging, MMS—21%
> Application downloads—18%

United Kingdom. After success with Magners Original Cider in the United Kingdom, Magners launched a brand extension called Magners Pear and used mobile to drive acceptance.[23] It created a mobile website that let consumers, with one click, locate a bar that served Magners Pear, and it added an option that allowed consumers to search for bars participating in free sampling promotions based on location. About forty-two thousand people searched for the bars, and three times more people clicked through the marketing message than the industry average.

Mexico. For its annual new product launch, Coty Adidas used mobile to introduce Fair Play, a fragrance for men. After a customer bought the cologne, he sent the first three digits printed on the box by SMS text message. Fifty percent of those who texted could win a prize, if they answered a question correctly, while the rest won mobile content. A quarter of the budget was assigned to mobile and there were more than four thousand prize winners, resulting in a significant increase in store sales of Fair Play.

Portugal. Leading retail chain Worten created a band challenge to discover future music stars, and used mobile to raise awareness of the brand and its stores. The company created a mobile site where unknown bands could register and upload their profiles, videos, and music. Consumers could then see those profiles, interact with them, vote, stream free music and videos, and win prizes. The mobile site attracted more than ten thousand visitors a week, resulting in more than a thousand daily music downloads and two hundred video downloads.

Hong Kong. Intercontinental Film Distributors of Hong Kong created a mobile campaign to promote the 3D animated film version of *Toy Story* in the Asia Pacific region.[24] The program used multimedia within the mobile content, allowing people to meet the characters of the movie, view trailers, and purchase tickets. The ultimate objective was to engage moviegoers and encourage them to purchase tickets from their phones.

Nigeria. Starfish Mobile and Glo—Nigeria's second-largest mobile operator, with more than twenty-five million subscribers—launched one of the largest mobile promotions in the area with a Bid2Win program involving a reverse auction. Mobile subscribers submitted bids by text message, and the lowest unique bid won a daily grand prize. The ninety-day campaign included a daily winner who received a car, and also awarded numerous other prizes.

Canada. To increase traffic and improve customer loyalty, the Vancouver company Glowbal Restaurant Group worked with the Tagga Agency to create a mobile program designed to update patrons on specials and promotions. The company had mobile text message information printed on items at the restaurant tables. Customers could text to receive special offers, such as discounts on meals and other specials made available only to mobile customers who received the message.

Luxury Brands and Mobile

As mobile grows in all parts of the world, it is also affecting companies and brands in all categories. This is especially true in luxury brands, some of which may have waited along the digital sidelines until the capacity arrived to electronically replicate the luxury brand experience. The reality is that, with all customers going mobile, luxury brands will be expected to enter that environment in one way or another.

One of the best-known luxury brands is Waterford Wedgwood Royal Doulton, known for an extensive range of crystal stemware, fine china, and other luxury home and lifestyle products. Because Waterford Crystal is the supplier of the crystal in the ball that drops in Times Square each year, the company created an iPhone app called Clink-Clink. Launched on New Year's Eve, the app allowed a person to select the desired crystal glass and do a virtual toast with another who performed the same action. As two phones "clinked" together, contact information could be instantly transferred between phones, if they were turned on. Otherwise, an individual could play the app, shake the phone, hear a clink, and see a different relevant saying each time.

After New Year's, Waterford expanded the app with tailor-made sayings for other holidays, such as Valentine's Day. That app event, triggered by the desire to leverage the New Year's Eve ball drop in a fun way, was only a small feature of a comprehensive long-term mobile strategy. In the last half of 2010, the company migrated its three major brands onto one platform on the Web before mobile-enabling the site. "As a brand, you have to broaden your strategy beyond the app because savvy customers will expect to also have a mobile-friendly interaction once they click on your logo or links within the app," says Leisa Glispy, Group Director of Global e-Commerce at Waterford Wedgwood Royal Doulton.[25] "We want to provide a luxury brand experience on all screens."

With new search capabilities, customers have more access to instant information at any given moment, even as they shop. Savvy marketers must be ready to provide useful information when customers want it, in a manner they expect from that company. "Mobile is changing the shopping experience," says Glispy. "You now have a more empowered customer who can comparison shop and share, on the go. Advancements in mobile devices will continue to change your customer experience, and companies need to be prepared to adapt to it. Your mobile strategy should integrate into your overall customer engagement strategy."

Another luxury brand that launched into mobile is Tiffany & Co., which created an app that allows high-end shoppers to view the settings, materials, and designs of engagement rings, including various stone shapes. It has a ring sizer that matches the size of a ring you place over the phone screen and a one-tap option that allows you to contact a Tiffany expert, and includes phone and e-mail contact information.

No matter the brand, every company in every category will have to find its own play in mobile, because their customers, no matter the demographic, are there.

Untethered consumers become totally empowered with features and functions that companies are making available to them via smartphones, a phenomenon we detail in the next chapter.

Smartphones Rule

It's not so much that cell phones are changing the world, but rather that smartphones are. During the computer revolution of the 1980s, the personal computer liberated people from the umbilical cord of the computer terminal connected to a centrally located and controlled mainframe. Personal computers allowed individuals to dramatically increase their personal productivity and performance. Each person could create and control his own documents, and breakthrough programs like Lotus 123, Excel, and Microsoft Word further empowered the individual.

A Computer for Every Hand

The next obvious technological step was to link computers through networks, so departments and entire organizations could share information and boost collective productivity. In the world of consumers, PCs expanded beyond the workplace, becoming common at home and school as well. Then came the global connectivity of the Internet, which rendered an unlimited amount of information available to anyone with a computer and a network connection.

In the midst of the PC revolution, the cell phone was born, though it was vastly different from the smartphone of today, which is basically a speaker, microphone, keyboard, display screen, circuit board with microprocessors, camera, GPS locator, and storage. It's basically a computer connected to a radio.

The Birth of the Cell Phone

On September 21, 1983, the first standardized cellular phone service was launched. That was the year that Motorola, after spending ten years and $100 million, introduced the DynaTAC 8000X mobile phone, the world's first commercial portable cell phone. The phone was referred to as "the brick," mainly because of its size and similarity to a brick (albeit light tan in color) with an antenna sticking out of the top. The phone battery could support one hour of talk time and eight hours in standby mode. It cost four thousand dollars. Many people became familiar with the phone when it was featured being used by Michael Douglas as Gordon Gekko in the movie *Wall Street*.

By 1986, there were two million cell phone subscribers, and the following year total cell phone revenue was $1 billion.[26] But those were truly the early years of cell phone use. A few years later, in 1989, Motorola launched the MicroTac cell phone, which introduced a flip-lid mouthpiece. The phone sold for three thousand dollars. This was finally a time when cell phones could be held in the palm of your hand and frequently were installed in cars, with many referring to the devices as "car phones." The next year, the number of cell phone subscribers topped five million, trivial compared to today's numbers.

In 1992, the first commercial text message was sent, and by 1996 there were thirty-eight million cell phone subscribers in the United States. The cell phone was starting to become more widely accepted as a part of daily life. A year later, the number of subscribers grew past fifty million and the digital wireless data and voice network known as 2G came into play. Cell phone use also continued to increase and in 1998, the average consumer used his phone for 122 minutes per month and two years later wireless subscribers in the United States topped 100 million. Today, well over 200 million people access Facebook from their mobile devices.

It was not until 2000 that camera phones were introduced in Japan and monthly phone use in the United States around that time increased to 320 minutes a month. And the growth of mobile did not stop there.

A few years later there were 180 million cell phone subscribers in the United States.

Over the course of just a few years, cell phone penetration in the United States jumped from 69 percent in 2005 to 94 percent in 2010, with a quarter of households using wireless phones only. And use dramatically increased as well, with cell phone minutes skyrocketing from 259 million minutes in 2000 to 2.3 trillion minutes in 2009.

Enter the Smartphone: The Two-Phone Era

In the middle of 2009, only 16 percent of mobile phone subscribers in the United States had a smartphone.[27] Just one year later that number had grown to a quarter of cell phone users, and by the end of 2011 the number is expected to be more than half.

What many people do not realize is that almost half of those with smartphones also have a regular cell phone.[28] Yes, they are carrying two phones. As you'll see later in this chapter, the same holds true around the world, with cell phone market penetration exceeding 100 percent in many countries, meaning that the number of cell phones is greater than the number of people in that country.

Demographically, the largest segment of smartphone owners is the twenty-five to thirty-four age group. In that segment, half have a smartphone only while the other half own both a smartphone and a regular mobile phone. The next largest group of smartphone owners are eighteen- to twenty-four-year-olds, followed by those thirty-five to forty-four years old. Of cell phone owners fifty-five to sixty-four years old, a fifth have a smartphone, with a portion of that group also owning both types of phones.

People with smartphones tend to be significantly more active using their phones, based on mobile research from InsightExpress. People with smartphones not only text more than those with regular phones, but six times more smartphone users browse the Internet by phone, three times more play games, ten times more use applications, and nine times more watch mobile video. Marketers will need to determine what their customers are doing with their phones before beginning to invest significantly in any particular segment of mobile marketing.

One of the reasons for such dramatic growth of smartphone use is that actions using the phone tend to be easier and more rewarding than on a non-smartphone or even a computer. More owners of smartphones considered using an application, playing games, listening to music, or watching videos a positive experience when they compared the smartphone to a feature phone.[29]

Consumers find smartphones easier to use, especially as they move in and out of Wi-Fi zones, which could affect speed. In fact, speed of loading is the number-one factor that determines whether a smartphone user will return to a mobile Web page. Next in importance are ease of navigation and quality and relevance of content. Since the actual experience or process of the experience supersedes the content or message in importance for smartphone owners, marketers have to first and foremost consider the mobile interactive experience.

Just Another Thing in My Pocket (vs. The Main Thing in My Pocket)

Smartphones come in various shapes and sizes, so the customer shopping for a phone for personal use gets to decide what she will carry. In many cases, though, corporations provide their employees with phones, which range from BlackBerry to Nokia models. This partly explains why many people have two phones; one may be supplied by the office, the other is for personal use. This two-phone setup may be dictated by corporate policies that allow the company phone to be used only for work; in some cases, the additional phone may reflect personal preference, that is, the individual prefers a phone other than the type the company issues.

Smartphones also are getting bigger, so that they better display pictures, video, and other multimedia. The Motorola Droid X, for example, is five inches long and more than two-and-a-half inches wide. The question many consumers will have to answer is, "What size phone do I want to carry?" That is, "Is the phone *just another thing in my pocket* or is it *the main thing in my pocket*?"[30]

The growth of smartphones is well documented and is expected to continue. The key driver of this growth is the functionality provided by smartphones. Customers can find information faster, they can receive personalized services based on their current location, and they can perform actions on their phones while on the go that they had previously done on their personal computers or other media devices.

Enter the iPhone Era

The turning point in mobile came with the launch of Apple's iPhone, with its following wave of hundreds of thousands of applications, which led to a dramatic increase in mobile Web browsing. The third-generation network, known as 3G, introduced higher-speed networking, which allowed Web surfing and audio/video transmission. As more fourth-generation networks (known as 4G) are deployed, with speeds five to ten times faster than the third generation, significantly more interactive data and video will move into the marketplace. This higher networking speed will combine with a new generation of computer processors that will speed smartphones even more. Smartphone sales will soon exceed sales of personal computers.

The impact of the iPhone in a world gone mobile cannot be over-stated. Many in the mobile industry—especially technology and platform providers—told us in the course of our research for this book that the introduction of the iPhone totally changed their business. We heard the same from both small and large brands, especially those that decided to create new applications and started by using the capabilities first provided by the iPhone.

"Fifty-five percent of Pandora's free listening is now done over mobile, and the iPhone doubled usage overnight," says Cheryl Lucanegro, Senior Vice President of Pandora, a personalized Internet radio service.[31] "Mobile changed our focus and strategy." Ironically, while the number of mobile users is well documented and well known, it took a number of years for advertisers to take note. "You have all your consumers there on mobile and you're devoting 2 percent of your ad budget there," says Lucanegro.

The iPhone showed not only what sophisticated phones could do, but how easy it is to download applications from a centralized location, the Apple App Store; funds could be automatically deducted from an iTunes account if the application required a fee, a setup already familiar to vast numbers of users who downloaded songs.

Many people were already comfortable using e-mail and other features from having used BlackBerry smartphones and other devices, but the iPhone, and then the Android operating system from Google, opened new vistas for what could be done from a mobile phone.

And mobile use, or at least capabilities using mobile, is evolving. For example, the so-called basic phone is fading into obscurity. Of the roughly third of cell phone users who own a basic phone, a full three quarters of them plan to upgrade to a phone with more advanced features, and a third plan for their next phone to be a smartphone.[32]

GLOSSARY

app. Short for application. Typically downloaded to a smartphone from an app store to enable the phone user to more easily accomplish a task. The task can range from checking the weather to comparing products and services.

app store. A service from which a user downloads an app; such services include Apple's App Store, Google's Android Market, and Research in Motion's App World (for BlackBerrys).

blindspots. Those customers who cannot be reached because of the limits of a particular campaign. For example, a campaign launched via an application that is available on Apple but not on Android, BlackBerry, or full-feature phones could cause a marketer to miss part of its target market.

branded app. Applications created typically by well-known brands to create an experience for the person who downloads it to his smartphone. One example is the Audi A4 Driving Challenge app, which lets a person race around various tracks, steering by turning the phone.

gestures. The sensors built into phones that facilitate changes, such as a screen automatically reformatting to landscape mode when turned sideways. Other examples include swiping, using two fingers to zoom in or shrink a page, pressing two phones together to transfer content, and shaking.

geotargeting. Method of determining physical location of a person and delivering content based on that location. The geographical targeting allows the marketer to send more relevant content.

NFC: An acronym for Near Field Communications, a short-range communication standard that allows the transfer of data between devices over a short distance (about four inches); it empowers a smartphone user to, among other things, convert his phone into a mobile wallet.

Swype: Technology that allows a person to drag his finger from character to character on a smartphone touch screen to spell a word or message rather than typing.

UPT: Abbreviation for Using Phone Technology, using the phone for marketing purposes but not capitalizing on the features of smartphones.

USPT: Abbreviation for Using Smartphone Technology. Involves utilizing features of smartphones, such as audio and video, applications downloads, high interactivity, m-commerce, image and bar code recognition, and location-based technology.

WAP: Wireless application protocol. Generally considered to be a website specifically formatted for display on a mobile phone (essentially, a mobile website).

The Platforms

As a marketer, one of the first issues you likely will hear about in mobile marketing is the issue of platform. As in traditional marketing, take care not to use purely anecdotal information to select a mobile strategy regarding platform. While it may seem obvious based on what you see and hear locally that *everybody* has either an iPhone or an Android-based phone or a BlackBerry, the real issue is what your customers are using. The first step is to answer ten questions about your customers' mobile characteristics:

1. What phones do my customers use?
2. What phones do my best customers use?
3. What phones do my potential customers use?
4. What mobile services do my customers use?
5. What are my customers doing with their phones?
6. What will my customers likely do with their phones in the future?
7. Do my customers use my website from their phones?

8. Do my customers send and receive text messages?
9. What percentage of my customers have smartphones?
10. What percentage of my customers expect to have smartphones, and when?

There are several different mobile platforms and, as a cell phone owner, you are likely familiar with at least one of them. The platform is essentially the operating system that makes the phone work. Just as there are PCs from companies like Dell and Hewlett-Packard that run one operating system, there are others from Apple that run another. Cell phones are similar, except there are more platforms and many suppliers of the mobile devices.

When it comes to the mobile phones themselves, hundreds of millions are sold each year. For example, in one three-month period last year, 111 million phones were sold just by Nokia, the top seller of phones globally.[33] The next leading companies, based on phones sold around the world by market share, are (in order) Samsung, LG, Research in Motion (makers of BlackBerry), Apple, HTC, and Motorola.

One consideration for reaching people via mobile phones is the region in which they live. For example, while Nokia is the leading manufacturer in Africa, Asia, and Eastern Europe, Apple leads in North America and Western Europe, based on one estimate.[34] And this mix is likely to change over time, as mobile growth is rapid and the market dynamics fluid, with continuous innovation driving adoption.

By platform, or operating system, the leaders around the world are, in order of market share, Symbian (Nokia), Research in Motion (BlackBerry), Android (by Google), iOS (by Apple), and Microsoft.[35] That picture also is evolving and is driven by various factors, ranging from features and capabilities to price and availability. And while the Android operating system from Google is available on a host of phones from companies such as Motorola and HTC, there is another operating system known as MeeGo project headed by Nokia and Intel.

When Internet use exploded globally, the variety of technologies was somewhat easier to deal with than it is in the mobile phone marketplace. The Internet operated via web browsers, most of which could access all information. Mobile has more moving parts, if you will. There are the phones themselves, the platforms, and the carriers, such as Verizon, AT&T, and Sprint, which provide service. But an application created for the Android operating system from Google does not necessarily work on Apple's iPhone, and vice versa.

The good news is that many mobile software companies have created technology that can transport content across multiple platforms. So as a marketer, platform compatibility ultimately will not be an obstacle for you, though it's an issue you should be aware of for the short term. More important will be your mobile marketing strategy and objectives; after you've set those, you can choose the technologies that will help you best achieve those objectives. As you will see throughout the book, there are technologies either currently available or in development that can solve almost any mobile marketing need. And some very well-known companies are pushing software developers to do even more.

Old vs. New Phones

There are essentially two ways to look at the mobile world as a marketer. You can reach only those with smartphones, and there are specific ways to do that, or you can reach those with almost any phone, and there are ways to do that as well. Throughout the book we show examples of both strategies, as implemented by a wide range of companies, well-known brands, and technology providers. The key questions are how, as a marketer, you want to reach your mobile customers and what you want to provide to them. There are two distinct ways to do this, ways we call UPT and USPT.

UPT (Using Phone Technology) simply means using technology that allows you, as a marketer, to reach customers through mobile phones. With UPT, you do not use the full features of a smartphone, such as location of the phone, for example. You also can deploy UPT to both types of phones. One example of UPT is sending text messages to a customer who has opted in to your marketing list, as most phones can receive such messages.

USPT (Using Smartphone Technology) involves utilizing features of smartphones, such as location-based technology or higher-end bar code scanning. It also could involve creating an app, which would be usable only on a smartphone but could deliver impressive features to those users.

For smartphones, a brand can create a mobile website, commonly referred to in the industry as WAP (wireless access protocol). Some companies with mobile websites are satisfied that they are reaching their customers with this approach and that their customers are receiving all the services and features they need and desire by this method.

However, mobile websites are not the only way to reach smartphone customers: companies can also create applications, or branded apps, that the customer easily downloads, making whatever functions are provided by the app available on the phone all the time. A common discussion within mobile marketing circles is whether to go "WAP or app," meaning whether to set up a mobile website or to create a customized app. A business can, of course, do both.

Smartphones are far more sophisticated than traditional cell phones, and have attributes that can be leveraged for marketing efforts:

Networking. Connected to the network all the time, by cell carrier or Wi-Fi, depending on location.

Location. Phone can be pinpointed by location at any time.

Camera. Photo and video resolution nearing or matching those of high-end cameras. Can stream video live to the Web or to a friend, or can save to memory.

Computing power. Small-sized but powerful computer.

Video. Can watch video in very high quality.

Motion. Can tell which way the phone is pointed, if it is shaken, and the type of motion made by the person moving it.

Touch screen. Highly sensitive to motions and other gestures.

Portable. Can (and likely does) go wherever its owner goes.

Voice. Still used for conversation, though some may forget this, with all the other capabilities the smartphone has.

Old Phone Money

While smartphones are clearly where the market is moving, there still is, and will continue to be, some marketing opportunity from the mass of phones around the world that are not so smart.

One company that has been extending its brand globally for many years is Chicago-based Playboy Enterprises, Inc. Founded by Hugh Hefner in 1953, the media company publishes *Playboy* magazine and creates content for distribution via television networks, websites, radio, and mobile platforms. Because it has licensing agreements around the world, the Playboy brand appears on consumer products in more than 150 countries.

The company understands traditional print models, still publishing twenty-nine international editions of its print magazine. It also understands the efficiency of the digital, mobile world compared with the publishing and distribution of its mainstay print property. "It may surprise you to know that our mobile business on average only nets 12 percent of retail or end user spend," says Greg Johnson, Director of Digital Ventures for Playboy.[36] "Once the operator, billing services provider, content aggregator, and distribution partners take their cut of the overall transaction, you're typically left with a fraction of the retail potential. I expect we'll continue to see the trend of content owners collapsing the value chain and moving to a more direct to consumer distribution model."

Johnson, who has worked at Playboy Enterprises for more than five years, led the company's mobile efforts until his role was expanded to include all digital ventures. Playboy's mobile division was treated as both an extension of its existing distribution channels as well as a revenue-generating vertical.

In the early days of mobile, when ringtones, wallpaper, and screen-savers were being sold by wireless operators, Playboy's trademark Rabbit Head Logo held the top spot with a North American Tier 1 operator for more than a year. That was the early business of mobile, simply buying sounds and pictures. "The Rabbit Head Design is one of the most iconic logos in history," says Johnson. In one year alone, the company sold more than five million downloaded wallpapers for mobile phones globally, generally at a ninety-nine-cent price point. "It's amazing to think that not long ago, operator decks were the primary source for purchasing content for your mobile phone," Johnson says. "The concept of the deck has been shattered by iPhone and Android. It's going to be interesting to watch the reorganization of content distribution from producer to consumer."

Playboy modified its strategy over time. "Playboy is in the midst of transition to a brand management company, focused on licensing one of the most powerful brands in the world rather than taking on overhead of operationally focused businesses," says Johnson. The company aligned with key strategic partners globally to ensure success in all facets of its mobile business.

"We're in the midst of an evolution in the publishing industry; I expect to see major changes in the way content is created, distributed, and consumed. Playboy's mobile division is poised to make a successful transition to brand management as a result of the strong mobile partnerships we've forged," says Johnson, who reviewed several mobile platforms before deciding on Mobile IQ in the United Kingdom. "It's like a flashback to the net in 1995," says Johnson. "The rules haven't been completely established. We're forging new ground and you're learning as you go, in many respects [this strategy relates to the test-and-learn concept, which we discuss elsewhere in the book]."

"We recently launched a pure mobile version of Playboy.com, and the site has the ability to adapt to visitors' devices in real time and present the best possible experience for each device. We're pleasantly surprised by the growth in traffic, number of page views, average time on site, and revenue," says Johnson. "There is clearly a pure mobile audience out there, and we expect to provide them an optimal experience while showcasing Playboy's premier content."

The Smarts of the Smartphone

Many people buy high-definition television sets but fail to take full advantage of the newfound power sitting in their living room. In many cases, consumers see so much improvement in the picture compared with their old set, they never sign up for the high-definition services offered by their cable or satellite TV operators. So while their picture is dramatically better than it was before, it could be exponentially better if they took advantage of the TV's capacity to show programs in true high definition.

A similar situation is occurring with smartphones. Just because smartphones exist doesn't mean all individuals or businesses will take advantage of all their capabilities. For example, while one in four people regularly use a smartphone, only one in six have apps on the smartphone they use.[37]

Much like a new high-definition TV, a new smartphone can be such an improvement over a previous regular phone that the new owner may not fully explore all of its features and capabilities. The good news for marketers is that this will change over time due to several drivers:

- Businesses will conduct research to determine what mobile customers most want.
- As network speed increases, features will be more easily accessed and used.
- App developers will continue to innovate.
- People will see others using functions they don't have and inquire about them.
- Customers will see the added value of using apps and mobile web features to make their lives easier.
- More businesses will enter the market to keep up with their competitors' offerings.

One of the key drivers of an increase in smartphone use is the availability of more and more apps that do an almost unlimited number of things. However, there are smartphone features that individuals use significantly more than they use apps. A study by Knowledge Networks shows that apps are a secondary consideration in general use of smartphones, following other features such as messaging, web use, search, and photography. Here's a breakdown of smartphone features regularly used, compiled by Knowledge Networks:

Phone calls	91%
Messaging	80%
E-mail	54%
Web/Internet	52%
Pictures/video	51%
Search	45%
Social media	38%
News/weather/traffic	31%
Apps	29%
Maps/directions	28%
MP3/digital music	28%
Games	27%
Video from TV networks	7%

For added perspective, the same study shows that when smartphone owners are shopping for a new phone or service, the variety of apps available is significantly less important than the overall capabilities of the service provider or the handset.

There is, however, a notable difference in usage patterns depending on the particular smartphone. For example, apps are used by 29 percent of smartphone owners overall; however, 77 percent of iPhone owners use apps regularly, a significant increase over other smartphone owners. While 18 percent of smartphone owners overall rated apps as very important, 36 percent of iPhone owners rate them as very important.[38] This is yet another reason marketers need to determine which mobile phones their customers use and what they do with them. Otherwise, a lot of money can be wasted on inefficient mobile marketing.

In addition to using a large number of apps, iPhone owners tend to have favorable opinions about advertisers who use apps. They are also more likely to use all the features of their phones than are owners of other smartphones. BlackBerry owners, the largest segment reported in the Knowledge Networks study, are often business users who may have a limited ability to download or use apps because of company policies. They also have fewer choices of apps, since there are significantly more iPhone and Android apps available.

Not all apps are free, though many are. While 64 percent of smartphone owners say they have an app on their phone, fewer than a third have any paid apps. It is more common for smartphone owners to download free apps, since they can try them and if not satisfied simply delete them with no cost. Once an app is paid for, the funds are typically not refundable, even if the user is not satisfied with the program. (Paid apps represent about a fifth of all apps.) Owners of iPhones are among the paying crowd, compared with owners of other phones. Almost three quarters of iPhone owners have paid apps compared with a quarter of those with Android phones and 14 percent of those with BlackBerry smartphones.

This issue of usage patterns is one of the elements marketers have to keep an eye on, and is partly based on what their customers are using for smartphones, if at all, and if so, which ones. Of course, this is only if you want to be involved in creating apps as part of your mobile marketing mix.

Brands and marketers can potentially derive revenue from apps, if they provide significant value. While many apps cost ninety-nine cents or $1.99, more than half of those who have bought apps have paid five dollars or more for at least one app, and almost a third paid ten dollars or more for at least one. A good example of a paid branded app is Kraft's iFood Assistant, which costs ninety-nine cents but allows customers to create shopping lists and to search menus. Sales of this app have shown that customers view the app as worth the money.

Spreading the Word on Apps

If, as a marketer, you decide that creating a branded application is the approach to take, you have to let people know about your app. This is much easier for a well-known and well-funded brand, which can add messages to its traditional marketing materials. However, it will be the value provided that will ultimately persuade the customer to download and use the app.

The most common way smartphone owners find out about new apps is by word of mouth, with almost a third learning of apps that way.[39] The remainder find out by searching, through social media, or, for iPhone users, via iTunes. What is not effective in marketing apps are television advertising, the web, or the phone itself. With the smartphone being such a highly interactive and personal device, it is only natural that word of valuable apps would spread in an organic way, through those who use them. If you create an app, it has to be good to be discovered and used.

This word-of-mouth transmission is another example of mobile being a pull rather than a push medium, with untethered consumers connecting to each other and sharing tips on what works for them. No longer is the marketer or brand in charge of broadcasting a message to the masses. In a world gone mobile, the masses are talking (and marketing) to each other.

The good news for marketers and brands is that customers with smartphones are open to marketing messages and are more inclined to buy from app advertisers compared with advertisers in various other media. For example, the Knowledge Networks study found that four out of five smartphone app users would be willing to view an advertising message on screen in exchange for a free app.

Another piece of good news for mobile marketers is that almost three quarters of smartphone owners consider advertising to be a fair price to pay for free downloads and use, a higher percentage than those who watch primetime television, view social media, or watch video on demand.

The iPad: The Lure of the Vanity Buy

When Apple launched its iPad in 2010, it instantly became the new bright, shiny object. Anyone who was anyone just had to have one. Those traveling with one on a plane got to show it off to others lugging those boring laptop computers and small smartphones. Because iPads were relatively scarce at first, those who owned one could feel special. They *were* special. It was the ultimate vanity buy, which is not a bad thing.

Advertisers committed about $60 million toward iPad advertising before many were even sold or any ads produced. Apple created iAd, a mobile advertising service intended to revolutionize advertising on the iPad (and iPhone). Within a few months, a few million iPads were sold, a successful launch.

The same phenomenon occurred with the introduction of Apple's iPhone 4, with owners of earlier iPhone models rushing to be the first to order the latest and greatest product, sight unseen. The iPhone 4 may have been another vanity buy, but because the products and product quality were breakthrough, the approach worked.

If a business can translate its core attributes into mobile, it can potentially create a product that will work as a vanity buy. The initial prompt to buy can be introduced by traditional advertising, such as full-page newspaper ads or TV commercials, but the mobile product ultimately has to deliver. A clue that a company is on the way to a vanity buy success is when one consumer is telling another, "Hey, look at this new app," or "Check this out," as he holds up his smartphone to show a friend.

A vanity buy, such as the iPad, is a "must want" rather than a "must have." It may not be critical to success or career advancement, but people sure want one.

The Push Behind Smartphones

One of the many reasons for the continuing growth of smartphone use is the push from the engines behind it and the platforms beneath it, which we'll discuss in greater detail as we move forward. But there are also technology hardware dynamics that help fuel the innovation that keeps the mobile industry moving forward. For example, an early generation of a smartphone may have limited storage space for apps and limited processing speed. This version would be leapfrogged by a newer smartphone with significantly more storage capacity or processing speed. Those shopping to replace a two-year-old smartphone will find dramatic improvements over the mobile device they may be retiring. In addition to the explosion of apps and the hardware improvements driving smartphones forward, there is the investment community, those funding much of the early mobile innovation.

Qualcomm Ventures formed and began funding companies in 2000 with a $500 million fund to make strategic investments in early-stage high-technology ventures. Since then, the company has funded many companies expanding into wireless and has set up additional funds in Korea, Japan, China, and Europe. The venture arm of Qualcomm looks for companies that provide both a strong potential return on investment and that complement existing Qualcomm products and services.

"Qualcomm is the Intel of the mobile world," says Nagraj Kashyap, Vice President and Head of Qualcomm Ventures.[40] "A large percentage of smartphones—Android, iPhone, RIM, Sprint, and Verizon—use Qualcomm chips. The chip used in the five-hundred-dollar netbook is the same chip used in the smartphone. The smartphone will be the de facto device by the end of the year. SMS (Short Message Service) will diminish once more people have smartphones." Companies like Qualcomm are funding and tracking the growth of segments of the mobile industry, in part so that they can leverage their own business interests.

Meanwhile, organizations such as CTIA Wireless and the Mobile Marketing Association help aggregate and support the mobile companies that provide the infrastructure, hardware, and software innovation as these mobile companies supply both major brands and small businesses looking to expand into mobile solutions for their customers.

Backers like Qualcomm are always looking ahead. "The industry is quickly moving in the direction of indoor," adds Jack Young, Senior Investment Manager at Qualcomm Ventures, referring to mobile companies that digitally map the interiors of buildings.[41] Such companies, which we describe later in the book, allow smartphone owners to locate specific stores in a mall or an airport, for example, in relation to the person with the smartphone. "With indoor, satellites get you within roughly ninety meters accurate."

"Qualcomm is working on the next generation Wi-Fi band triangulation, to get you within ten meters accuracy. Now I know where you are within ten meters. Then there is geospatial location. That is, here's the map. In this case, advertising becomes dollars per pair of feet. I know precisely where you are in the store. The marketer now can close the loop." The implications of this could be significant for marketers, allowing them to more accurately determine the location of potential customers in relation to stores or even specific products. Because many advertisers want to reach customers close to the actual purchase decision, this more precise targeting technology, in conjunction with the proper privacy and business models, could potentially allow advertisers and brands to work within new pricing structures. For example, pricing for an ad might be based upon how many people act on the message by making a purchase at the time and place the message is delivered.

Young sees continued growth in mobile advertising, because people will be spending more time viewing their third screens. "Advertising will find ways to get in," he says. "There will be more relevance because display ads can be more targeted and more intimate."

With the innovation in the mobile industry and the constantly flowing content, mobile drives customers and marketers toward more of a real-time environment than has ever been possible, an area we explore in the next chapter.

Real Time Moves to All the Time

The mobile consumer never sleeps. Well, at least they don't all sleep at the same time. Consumers at televisions and computers take a break. They physically get up and leave the device, or they turn it off. Not so with mobile. In a world gone mobile, all information is available to all, all the time, creating new business challenges, including how to market in real time and how to market all the time.

The original concept of real time carried with it the implication that a transaction could be immediate, but that it was company-driven, so that the real time would be the actual time people were there at their computers. In the third screen revolution, real time becomes all the time, with untethered consumers expecting to be able to act and interact in a true 24-7 environment; the phone is always there. With all-the-time expectations, consumers are driving companies to modify cycles of development, creation, production, and delivery of products and services so that they more closely reflect the needs of the always-on mobile consumer. And those needs are totally on the customer's timeframe.

Information Resides in the Smartphone "Cloud"

Just as printed newspapers became less relevant as a source of news and information because of the Internet, the third screen will transform the way that information is gathered and shared. In the third screen revolution, information becomes dynamic and resides in cyberspace. So-called *cloud computing*, where information resides on dynamic networks on the widely scattered servers of companies like Google, Microsoft, and IBM, is quickly becoming the engine of mobile computing.

Untethered consumers store information such as calendars and contacts on these networks and expect to be able to access their information from any location. The challenge for businesses is to make information about their products and services available at all times in this mobile computing model, and to keep the information dynamic and constantly up to date. Untethered consumers who are shopping expect to access inventory databases directly to see who has what products at what price at any given moment. Some companies have figured this out and are starting to make this data available to mobile customers.

Habits have evolved over many years, as the technology of the time dictated activities in media or content consumption at particular times. In the early days of radio, a program followed a certain schedule, and the consumer or even the entire family chose to listen to a specific show at the scheduled time. It was a time commitment on the part of the consumer, but that time slot was selected by others—the programmers or station operators.

Along came TV, and the time-based model remained largely intact. Networks broadcast shows at certain times, and it was determined that the best shows would run in prime time, the evening hours after dinner. This model endured globally, with varying official starting times, depending on the country. The large audiences that gathered at one time provided the greatest opportunity for companies to reach consumers through network advertising, which remains a multibillion business today. Special globally broadcast shows (World Cup Soccer, Super Bowl, etc.) attracted even wider audiences, commanding more advertising dollars as marketers were provided with an opportunity to reach masses of people all at one time.

Key in all these activities is that the broadcasters, stations, and advertisers controlled the time. If you missed the scheduled broadcast, you may have lost your chance to view the program, or you had to wait patiently for a rerun at what again may not have been a convenient time.

The introduction of the videocassette recorder (VCR) started to slowly move time control to the consumer, allowing her to time shift by taping a program or movie and watching it when *she* wanted rather than when the network chose to broadcast it. This was followed by the digital video recorder (DVR), which did essentially the same thing as the VCR but used digital technology, making it easier for research companies such as Nielsen and Arbitron to measure actual viewer numbers and times.

Marketers and advertisers wanted to reach particular demographics or market segments at certain times, and these measurement services let them know how well they were doing that. Americans spend more than nine and a half hours a month watching time-shifted programs, deciding when *they* want to watch the shows.[42] The key here is that consumption of content transitioned so that it became more under the control of the individual.

TiVo added a slightly different twist to the DVR by using technology to predict which shows a consumer might like based on past shows he had watched, and then recording those as-yet-unwatched shows automatically. Meanwhile, the growth of cable television channels in the U.S. market increasingly segmented audiences, making it more challenging for marketers to reach large, sought-after demographics in one place at one time.

An explosion of Internet use introduced a dramatic new time component that allowed those with computer and network connections to not only interact but also seek content to consume or view on their own time, while they were at the computer. While popular TV shows still aired in traditional prime time, consumers were gradually shifting so that they had greater control over their viewing. They were leaning forward even more, as online video continued its magnetic pull:

- More than 135 million people in the United States watched online video in one month in 2010.[43]
- The average viewer watched more than seventy-two video streams in a month.

- The average viewer spent 190 minutes watching video in one month.
- More than 100 million people watched a YouTube video within one month.

The pull of video led to new behaviors and habits of consuming via the computer. The introduction of Hulu in 2007, by owners including The Walt Disney Company, NBC Universal, and News Corp., allowed consumers to watch even more traditional television programming on their computers. The online video service offers hit shows, clips, and movies from many content companies, such as MGM, National Geographic, Fox, PBS, and Warner Bros. Rather than being a passive recipient of content, held captive by the dictates of the networks, the consumer could now reach out and pull content to them, on *their* timeframe.

The model began to change from broadcasting, controlled by the information broadcaster, to what I call *pull-casting*, controlled by the information-pulling consumer. But the restriction of location still existed. While consumers could pull content and consume it when they wished, they could do it only while in front of their TV or PC.

Mobile completes the movement toward consumer time control by freeing the viewer from location limits; the viewing device is literally in the hands of the consumer, giving him nearly total access to content at any time and place. Broadcasting to mobile devices will still occur, though it will involve different dynamics than traditional broadcasting, including time-based marketing and new methods of targeting and measurement.

Real-Time Bidding for Marketing Messages

One of the companies that helps facilitate the move to real-time marketing, at least for publishers, is AdMeld. Founded in 2007, the company services more than 300 of the world's leading online publishers, using its technology to connect them with every major buyer and giving the publishers control over how they sell their inventory, to whom, and at what price. The focus of the company, which is headquartered in New York with offices in San Francisco, London, and Toronto, is to increase advertising revenue of the publishers.

The aggregate reach of all the publishers using AdMeld is more than 400 million unique users worldwide, with about 200 million of those in the United States. Its publisher clients include AccuWeather, Fox News, Discovery Communications, Hearst Television, IAC, *The New York Post*, Answers.com, and World Wrestling Entertainment.

Consistent with the move from real time to all the time, AdMeld supports Real-Time Bidding (RTB), so that its publishers can make it easy for marketers to reach the right person with the right message over the right mobile network at the right time. The significance of this real-time buying and selling is a change in the pricing dynamics of advertising. Messages can be highly targeted to certain untethered customers at the highest moment of value, increasing the effectiveness—and thereby the price—of the marketing message. Marketers win because their messages are more efficient and publishers win because they fetch higher rates from the advertising. Mobile makes this all possible.

AdMeld recognizes the significance of mobile's role, especially because of its real-time nature. "Location-based advertising is only possible through RTB," says Marc Theermann, Vice President of Mobile at AdMeld.[44] "Google does RTB with search, essentially. Real-time bidding will be significant in the ecosystem of mobile. Traditional ad networks are not doing it."

AdMeld registers more than a billion views a month from mobile devices as advertising is being auctioned in real time, and the company sees mobile growing dramatically. "The consumer is already there in scale, the advertisers are not," says Theermann. "General business is not as engaged as they should be. Mobile is not easy and it's hard for a single business to do. They have to decide, do I want to be on Android or iPhone? Any mobile company needs to shield the business from the confusion."

One of the growth areas around mobile centers around retail, where customers armed with mobile phones can easily aggregate. "Retailers can engage with consumers," says Theermann. "But there are some complex issues. It involves payment, research, loyalty, and manual or automatic check-in, for example."

The age-old question still on the minds of many is whether custom-ers will accept advertising on their phones. "If you ask consumers, they say no to ads," says Theermann. "That was true in every medium. But the American public has shown a tremendous resilience to advertis-ing. Mobile is about a medium for dialogue and direct response. If you engage the customer, and they locate their friends who are like you, real-time bidding can provide a value."

A company's success in the mobile revolution requires that it provide distinct value to its mobile customers, wherever they are and based on their needs at the moment. With the third screen, the traditional broadcasting model will not work. In the environment of the m-powered consumer, customers will find and watch what they want to watch, and it may be over the course of a day rather than over the course of thirty or sixty minutes. When it comes to video on mobile, marketers need to think in terms of smaller and shorter. That means short videos, quick messages, high interactivity, and value to the customer.

Starting with Research

The Nielsen Company is a global information and media company noted for its marketing and consumer data collection and research, television and other media measurement services, and mobile and online measurement services, as well as its trade shows and business publications. The privately held company is headquartered in New York and is active in about a hundred countries.

Paul Kultgen is the director of Mobile Media and Advertising for Nielsen, where he leads a team that deals with the media aspects of businesses, such as advertisers, advertising agencies, and ad networks. His group, which has been measuring mobile for more than ten years, provides research and advice regarding strategy, consulting, recom-mendations, media planning, buying tools, and effectiveness measure-ment. Like many others involved in mobile, Kultgen recommends that businesses considering mobile carefully research their customers' hab-its and mobile use. "On any media channel, it starts with the question of whether there is research to it," says Kultgen.[45] "With mobile, it's not like online, it's not one media channel. It's a multifaceted, multimedia channel. The challenge with mobile is to make sure it's representative, since there are device considerations, carriers, and more. Emerging media is tough to measure. It's like 1995, when companies were asking 'Should I put a URL on my ad?'"

Kultgen advises businesses to ask themselves several key questions specific to their customers.

- Is there general agreement that mobile use is at critical mass for our customers?
- What is the potential to reach our market? What is our particular market doing with mobile?
- What phones are our customers using? Smartphones are becoming the predominant handset, but not all smartphones are created equal.

Tying your strategy to your specific customers' preferences is critical when launching a mobile marketing effort. "For example, your company may find that the majority of your customers use a particular phone, such as iPhone or BlackBerry," says Kultgen. "This can help determine which messages are created for which platform, at least initially, to ensure reaching the largest number of current or potential customers. We're telling clients you have to place your bets. BlackBerry still has a dominant user base tied to the Enterprise. Lots of marketers are carrying two phones, one for work and one for personal use. This makes it challenging for BlackBerry."

In the traditional TV broadcasting model, advertising is a key component and consumers have been trained over many years to accept commercials and various advertising messages. In the early phases of mobile, consumers will again be subject to a training process for accepting advertising messages, as marketers work to determine the most effective methods for mobile marketing.

"Only 10 percent of people say ads on mobile are acceptable," says Kultgen. "If you look at richer media, it is more acceptable. No one says they want advertising but they all accept it. The idea of advertising needs to be linked to the brand experience you're creating. What utility or enrichment are you providing? With smartphones, the key is if more of the capabilities can be realized. LBS (location-based services) are a component of that."

Part of the mobile experience will involve broadcast, although the audience selection process will be far different than with the traditional model, in which an individual turned on a TV to watch a particular show. The mobile consumer is frequently in motion, and not necessarily predisposed to advertising messages simply converted from other media. In addition, there are different aspects of mobile that need to be considered, including technological aspects and modes of interactivity. Says Kultgen:

> Mobile is complex. Unlike online, there's a real technical side to mobile. There are a lot of moving parts. Everyone wants to put it into a bucket they know. Mobile is game changing. It is new media and a new channel. People need to get their heads around it. You don't have a lot of mobile marketing experts out there. There's a constant struggle.
>
> In mobile the focus is, "What is my brand's presence and how do I use the channel?" Everyone wants everything measured. The big challenge in measuring is how you measure mobile across media. There's loyalty, purchase decision, and more.
>
> It needs to be about a bigger brand experience and getting value through mobile interaction. It's about utility and enrichment. The Kraft app [an application by Kraft Foods that features recipes, shopping lists, and more] is a good example. Not many people take a computer into the kitchen, but mobile they will. And banking has done a good job.
>
> It's not about a coupon. Mobile dies if the only interaction is discounting. Couponing needs to play a role. Why is anyone talking paper coupons when you have a phone? You need to make mobile a call to action. Ultimately, push is where it's going to happen, but the consumer is going to have to opt in. You need push for scale but consumer pull needs to provide the value.
>
> It's extremely challenging for a brand to do an app with something like three hundred thousand apps available. The Krafts of the

world were rewarded for being early. They were very smart in how they marketed their app.

Consumers are leading most marketers. Consumers are moving faster than marketers are. In mobile it's about advertising versus marketing a customer brand experience. The Kraft iFood experience is a good example. It isn't just about advertising, it's about enhancing the brand experience.

First-move advantage wins. Like in retail, how do you integrate mobile in the store? If you were a big advertiser and said, "I'll put 1 percent of my budget into mobile," it would be huge.

Research on mobile activities can be a very powerful tool for analyzing any given market segment, and can help you determine the most effective types of marketing messages for the majority of those customers. In addition to advance research, businesses also need to experiment with what works with their particular customers in real time, because customer reaction remains the best measure of marketing effectiveness. Mobile marketing relies on the test-and-learn philosophy.

Dealing with Customers in Real Time

Mobile innovation can come from almost any place or any organization. While a robust and growing mobile industry continues to fuel the technological power behind the mobile revolution, there are innovators at well-known brands leading the charge inside their respective companies. Driving through the heart of Queens, New York, to a large factory and office building in the midst of a residential area in Long Island City leads to one such company.

Steve Madden Ltd. is a two-decades-old leading designer and marketer primarily of women's shoes, handbags, and accessories. The company sells millions of pairs of shoes a year through its own retail stores, its e-commerce–focused website, department and specialty stores throughout the United States, and various distributors in Canada, Europe, Central and South America, Australia, and Asia.

At one end of an expansive set of offices is a large room where shoe and accessory designers conceive of and create the latest footwear trends. Drawings and sketches of shoes are abundant. Craftspeople take the latest ideas and convert them into reality. Around the corner is a much smaller room just as lively, packed with computer screens, white boards, and bulletin boards filled with ideas. This is the technology innovation center that helps take the value created in the larger room and connect it directly to the untethered consumer. This is the home of the e-commerce team and the heart of Steve Madden Ltd.'s move to mobile. In these offices are craftspeople in their own right. "I immediately realized how powerful and transformative mobile would be," says Andrew Koven, President of E-Commerce and Customer Experience at Steve Madden Ltd.[46] "Smart retailers are moving from a culture of doing business in multiple silos or channels to becoming fully integrated multichannel enterprises where the customer is at the center of the model."

Koven is not a newcomer to the digital interactive world, having witnessed the birth of e-commerce. He was Vice President of Business Development and Customer Relationship Management at ShopLink, a pioneer in the online grocery business, and Chief Marketing Officer of Fresh Direct in 1999. Koven realizes his early experience is a great benefit and easily sees the differences between marketing then and now. "With mobile commerce, the ramp is a lot quicker because it's being driven by the consumer," he says. "It took ten years for e-commerce to take hold, and m-commerce will do it in three. There are game-tested retail executives who grew up on e-commerce, direct marketing, and one-to-one customer experience building. We know where to focus our time and resources to achieve results."

The company's mobile strategy is highly focused and customer-centric, employing a crawl, walk, run approach. With the target market composed of fashion forward, lifestyle-oriented girls and women in their late teens through early forties, Koven realized that the Steve Madden customer was inherently mobile. "Our customers are amazing, very loyal, passionate, engaged, and active communicators," says Koven.

Koven openly admits that he found himself in the right place at the right time with the right people internally to seize the opportunities. However, developing the company's mobile strategy was far from simple. If the mobile deployment was faulty, it would reflect negatively on the brand and potentially impact sales.

Koven broke down the company's mobile strategy into seven separate components:

- **Assessment.** Defining the business requirements and statistics.
- **Departmental.** Deciding which departments need to be involved. At a minimum, these are E-Commerce, IT, Marketing, Finance, and Legal.
- **Process.** Managing the project, including: hosting, testing, security, calendar, go-live strategy, data collection methods, vendor selection, and contracts.
- **Testing.** Assessing analysis and reporting, usability, and systems, as well as e-commerce vulnerability testing, load testing, mobile environment testing, and uptime testing.
- **Soft Launch.** Introducing the mobile site to a limited audience and assessing site management.
- **Formal Launch.** Launching with features including SMS, WAP site, QR Codes, and click-to-call capabilities.
- **Mobile Marketing and Data Analysis.** The technology and tools to create the tracking systems to monitor mobile success.

When considering how to leverage the power of untethered consumers, one of the primary issues is understanding your customers' current and future use of mobile, their needs, and how your company can fulfill those needs via their mobile phones and devices such as the iPad and iTouch. Although this may sound simple, there are multiple aspects that organizations should tackle before launch, many of them internal. In the case of Steve Madden Ltd., Koven identified a series of questions that had to be addressed, including:

- How do we support a new and more efficient research and buying process?
- What channels of business are the beneficiaries? Stores, e-commerce sites, wholesale partners?
- What are the data collection and synchronization considerations?

- What features and functions does the mobile commerce site have to provide?
- How can mobile benefit the customer experience?
- What level of investment should be made to launch successfully—and how do we measure success and ROI for such an early-stage initiative?
- What support is needed from IT (Information Technology)?
- How do we integrate to all channels of sales?
- What could the new model for customer engagement and service look like?
- What are the training considerations for store associates, who will need to assist highly informed and empowered consumers?
- How do we integrate social engagement with mobile?

Making the Case for Mobile Internally

Koven had to justify for himself, as well as to other company leaders, the reasons to invest in mobile. Along the way, he learned lessons that may be useful for other businesses. Says Koven:

> Look at the minutes spent on mobile. If you're getting engagement, you're influencing sales. Not everything can be quantified in terms of direct ROI. I prefer an attribution to the entire enterprise approach.
>
> Present the practical, historical, and competitive cases. It's like asking ten years ago, "Why do we need a website?" I look at what I'm doing, what kids today are doing, and probably what you're doing. In one form or another, most are doing something via mobile.
>
> Mobile, like no other channel before it, is poised to influence billions of dollars a year in retail sales as an industry. It's my responsibility to ensure that Steve Madden is positioned to succeed.

Koven has built an e-commerce team of more than fifty members, including those in merchandising, IT, customer service, direct marketing, photography, and web design. Rather than increasing the size of the e-commerce group to move into mobile, he leverages staff throughout the organization and works closely with his partners. He tests everything in mobile internally before rolling it out. "It's a constant test-and-learn mentality when it comes to mobile. And in the case of mobile innovation at Steve Madden, we've got lots of strong ideas. It's not beyond the realm for someone to get a call from me in the middle of the night with an idea or question."

One innovation came to fruition when a member of the marketing team at Steve Madden suggested adding the Facebook "Like" option to the e-commerce site. Koven immediately jumped on it for the mobile site. The feature allows any shopper on the mobile site to tap or click one button to show that they like a particular product. The "Like" was then automatically posted to the person's Facebook Wall so all their friends would see it. This was the first known use of Facebook's "Like" feature on mobile. The "Like" feature was then expanded to product recommendations and the Steve Madden brand.

The result has come to be known as SoMo, or social mobile. Mobile shoppers could now let their friends know instantly, at the point of experience, what products they liked. For example, if a person liked a particular shoe, she could easily and quickly share that piece of information with all her friends. According to Koven, "Social mobile creates viral energy and excitement. We recognized that a lot of people were updating Facebook by phone, including ourselves. It was a no-brainer. But the real win is the long-term transformative effect that SoMo is going to have on our level of responsiveness as a company. Social commerce enables the consumer to tell us where we cleared the bar and also where we're missing it. It's on us to respond, and Steve Madden has a very responsive culture."

Koven, validated by mobile response, decided to add the "Like" feature to the company's e-commerce site per his marketing partner's recommendation. When the "Like" feature was added to the mobile commerce site, the Facebook page had 16,800 fans. The company is projecting more than a hundred thousand fans by the end of 2011 with several times more product "Likes" And powerful fan engagement.

On the Facebook fan page, Koven's e-commerce and marketing teams create competitions between different shoes, handbags, and accessories; feature new products, Steve Madden music artists, personal appearances; and more. In the case of one competition, the first shoe to receive a thousand Facebook "Likes," which was tested on mobile, would receive a special offer for twenty-four hours. The promotion increased mobile site traffic by 30 percent in one day. The logic was simple. A person's friends would see what they liked, attracting more attention to that product and causing even more people to view it and vote. The market determines the top-rated shoe based on votes, and the company gains the benefit of our fans' energy and feedback.

With Steve Madden Ltd.'s social mobile effort, the company provides the mobile platform and communication forum and the customer provides the content. This is one of the key leverage points of mobile—to facilitate real-time engagement, immediate communication, and interaction between customers and the brand.

Koven is also testing location-based social networking services, including Foursquare (which we'll discuss further later in the book); if a customer "checks in" he receives a coupon code that can be used to purchase shoes. Koven also partnered with location-based service Loopt, so that anyone who checks in at any of Steve Madden's stores can receive a 20 percent discount on any purchase of fifty dollars or more for a limited time.

After a rigorous search, Koven selected Branding Brand out of Pittsburgh, Pennsylvania, to collaborate with and to build their mobile commerce platform. The company used its Echo Technology, which translates the Web commerce content and capabilities of Steve Madden onto mobile while also allowing for customized features. By using the echo approach, Koven eliminated any significant handling needs by his IT department, since a change on the Web automatically transferred to mobile. One of the custom features on mobile that he is excited about is the real-time store lookup of inventory so customers could instantly see where a product is available based on their geo-location.

Koven recognizes that the general marketplace is moving to smartphone adoption. He found that he could cater to smartphone users within a WAP environment, supplying just about any functions needed by customers without developing a special branded application. In doing so, he makes the mobile experience available to the widest audience. Steve Madden's mobile site includes a large number of best practice features, including keyword and visually aided search, deep linking, search filtering, slide-down menus and sizing charts, product images and multiviews, product alternatives, recommendations, jump-to features, breadcrumbs, social integration, send-to-a-friend, and store inventory lookup by geolocation. Product reviews are coming shortly.

The shopping cart function was integrated with the e-commerce website, including log-in, promotional code, and order tracking features. If a customer wants to view the entire website from mobile, there is also a one-touch option for that. The entire budget for the mobile e-commerce launch was in the $150,000 to $200,000 range. Koven says, "With mobile, you can and should leverage your existing assets."

In the first month after launch, the mobile-optimized site received fifty-five thousand visitors, had 340,000 mobile views, and received 450 orders for merchandise. The following month, the number of mobile visitors more than doubled, to 117,142, with 497,000 mobile views and 908 orders. Koven also tracks statistics on virtually every aspect of mobile interaction including time spent and products sold. For example, he routinely monitors data such as the following:

- Average time spent on mobile site: 6.5 minutes per visitor
- Time spent on mobile site in one day: 36,800 minutes across all visitors
- Over one million minutes a month spent on the mobile site
- Fewer mobile pages seen but more time spent on mobile
- Three million minutes spent on first hundred days of mobile site
- Top driver of revenue is the iPhone; BlackBerry is number four
- For customer service, 7 percent use click-to-call
- Sales conversion is 1 percent
- 56 percent visit store locator feature

Koven launched Steve Madden Ltd's mobile site in the middle of 2010, and he has some thoughts and questions about the cultural shifts necessary for retail success in the future:

One of the more common questions retailers will need to address is what to do if [the company's] product is cheaper elsewhere. How will salespeople be trained to deal with such on-the-spot mobile-caused scenarios in a store with a customer in front of them? Here are a couple of lessons learned along the way: Retailers and brands should recognize that mobile done well improves sales for a multichannel retailer. It feeds the entire business. It's not about cannibalization, it's about total enterprise performance improvement. That being said, if a retailer is not aligned culturally and preparing systematically, it will struggle to compete long term.

With mobile, the length of time spent browsing is shorter and pages a bit fewer. Consumers are more focused with regard to their intent. Our goal is to ensure that the customer can achieve their information gathering and shopping goals easily and efficiently. Relevance is no longer a concept, and good information rules the day. Mobile marketing, which includes customer service, must demonstrate that I listened to what my customers told me and responded to what they asked for, in a timely manner. With mobile, the sense of urgency has increased.

Imagine mobile replacing the consumer's wallet and it will. Consumers look at their pictures, shop, check the weather, manage their calendars and finances, update their Facebook status, make and receive phone calls, book travel, and more. In terms of mobile thought leadership, it's incumbent upon us to be where our customers are today and take them where they want to go.

Koven is following the success of Steve Madden's mobile launch by building a mobile database; supported by online and in-store advertising, he's inviting customers to join the Steve Madden mobile club. The incentives to participate will include exclusive content, contests, and special offers sent directly to the mobile phone. When someone sends a text message to join, she receives a message back welcoming her to the club with a request to add personal information and preferences. Once the information is submitted, she receives on her phone a personalized thank you message.

And because Steve Madden is also known for music, the company will look into utilizing its in-store video monitors to send featured Steve Madden Music artists' videos to customers' phones, once they opt in. The video, of course, includes the opportunity to buy the shoes featured in the video.

Koven had additional thoughts on the future of mobile marketing. "SMS and MMS are perfect for in-store mobile expansion," he says. "It's a reverse engineering of the traditional marketing model, where the customer is now driving the level and type of engagement that works for them."

Using mobile for research, Steve Madden customers will be able to vote on future designs of shoes, handbags, and apparel by texting the label A, B, C, or D to a number provided. To extend brand loyalty to mobile, Koven conceived of the idea, which he hopes to implement in the future, to add text message information to Steve Madden packaging, allowing customers to register their purchase, regardless of where it was bought. "The possibilities are endless," says Koven. "That being said, we're going to maintain our mobile focus on driving results by ensuring it's fun and easy to do business with us."

By the end of six months, more than 10 percent of the total web traffic to Steve Madden came from mobile, which grew 250 percent over six months. More than half a million dollars worth of merchandise sold over mobile during that period.

In many ways, the Steve Madden approach to mobile marketing is a microcosm of what is here today and what is coming in mobile's future:

- The initial approach was pragmatic, with consistent test-and-learn activities.
- The company took a USPT approach, leveraging the location capabilities of smartphones so that customers could find the most appropriate products in relation to their location.
- The company included calls to action throughout its customer interactions.
- The company measures everything, including overall sales, the products that sell, and which customers buy which products at which locations.
- The system allows customers to easily opt in and opt out of its mobile platform.

- The company tracks its customers in terms of the phones and features they use.
- It markets in place, where the customer is at the moment.

The Mobile Time-Shifting Conundrum

One way for you to gauge how much time people are connected via their phones is to take a look around the office at your colleagues. You're likely to notice that executives and managers are almost never without their cell phones. You can see people attempting to discreetly check their phones for messages during meetings. Sometimes they glance at their phones while you're talking to them, just for that split second. Maybe they think you won't notice if the look is fast enough. Maybe you've done it as well, on occasion.

The key is that they're taking care of these tasks within their own timeframe, when they want to. It's not while sitting at a computer. It might be while taking an escalator or walking down a hallway. No matter the location, it is at a time of their choosing. The person sending the message cannot determine when the recipient will view it, though it may arrive instantly.

Why would the mobile behavior of your customers be any different from that of your colleagues? It's probably not. People dip in and out of their phones and the content on those phones on a continual basis. This move to real time, all the time, has many implications for marketing. The mobile customer now drives the timing.

People at work are glued to their mobile phones (See our survey: Time Without a Phone). On a typical day the majority of business leaders (54 percent) spend less than an hour a day without their phones, and more than a third of them (36 percent) have their cell phones turned on and with them at all times during their waking hours.[47] These figures are not driven by size of company, as those working in both small and large companies spend similar amounts of time without their cell phones.

"Relying on mobile technology has become a survival tool, like a Swiss Army Knife," says one manager, "For e-mail, web services, directions, and advice on where to eat, I would have to relearn how to live without it."

SURVEY: TIME WITHOUT A PHONE

On a typical day during all your waking hours, how much time are you without your cell phone (it is turned off, not with you, etc.)?

None 36%

Up to 1 hour 18%

Up to 2 hours 11%

Up to 3 hours 10%

Up to 4 hours 6%

Up to 5 hours 3%

Up to 6 hours 4%

7 or more hours 9%

Do not use a cell phone. 3%

VOICES FROM BUSINESS: WITH PHONE

Following are comments from respondents to the above survey.

"I have two: a company-issued cell and a personal cell, both of which are always on."

"Most senior execs, especially those with global operations, have cell phones on 24-7."

"Crackberry Nation is what we are."

"The phone is with me, or within reach, except during sleeping hours."

"Most of my contacts know that I'm nearly always around a way to check my e-mail. IM is the second next preferred way to communicate."

"Having the ability to be more mobile (out of office) but still be functional and productive is liberating if you allow it to be that way. The alternative is to become a slave. The difference is that you take control of how you use the phone."

"I use my cell phone for everything. It's my alarm clock, scheduler, Internet, pager, blackbook. It's Windows-based so I can see spreadsheets, send e-mail, see Outlook. If I don't have it, I am lost."

"The technology of the iPhone allows me to constantly monitor work and personal items without being intrusive on my valuable family and friend time. I have experienced much less stress as a result of remaining current and up to date."

"The smartphone is my lifeline to the business for e-mail, SMS and apps. It is always on."

Mobile Phone Usage

So what are all those people in business doing with their phones while at work? The top cell phone uses for business leaders while working are talking (89 percent), receiving e-mail (74 percent), sending e-mail (70 percent), and texting (61 percent). What they are doing least on cell phones while working is watching video or using social networks, including Twitter, LinkedIn, and Facebook.

When not working, business leaders use their cell phones in much the same way that they do while working. The top uses are talking (93 percent), receiving e-mail (74 percent), sending e-mail (74 percent), and texting (69 percent). By title, a larger percentage of senior executives than managers use their mobile phones to browse the Web and view information such as sports and news.

When not working, these same executives and managers use their cell phones a little differently. While the top use is talking, managers and executives use their cell phones almost equally for texting and e-mail.

Compared to the same survey conducted the previous year, Web browsing while at work increased from 29 percent to 41 percent.

Following are the survey questions to senior executives and managers in order of results.

While working, I use my cell phone for the following (check all that apply):

Talking 89%

Receiving e-mail 74%

Sending e-mail 70%

Texting 61%

Web browsing 41%

Getting information (news, sports, etc.) 39%

Photos. 24%

Facebook. 16%

LinkedIn 120%

Twitter. 9%

Video. 9%

While NOT working, I use my cell phone for the following (check all that apply):

Talking 93%

Receiving e-mail 74%

Sending e-mail 74%

Texting 69%

Getting information (news, sports, etc.) 52%

Web browsing 50%

Photos. 45%

Facebook. 25%

Video. 21%

LinkedIn 16%

Twitter. 11%

VOICES FROM BUSINESS: USE OF PHONES AT WORK

Following are comments from respondents to the previous survey.

"With every opportunity to stay plugged in, when are you not working in today's business environment? When not working I check e-mail, etc., as do all in my company."

"Company very strict on how you use company phone. No texting, twitter,' 411,' web browsing. When I am not working I use my personal phone to do at will."

"I don't live 'n die by my cell phone. I use it to access weather for aviation planning, check e-mail on the road, and make telephone calls."

"My cell phone has blurred the lines between working and not working. Generally, if I'm checking it, I end up working."

"Hard to walk away from the BlackBerry, even in the evenings and weekends."

"Having access to e-mail on the go helps in keeping the message queue under control. Also helpful in traveling to keep up with what's going on in the office. I can always make use of those 'wasted minutes' waiting in line, sitting in a waiting room, waiting for a meeting to start, etc."

"I would be totally lost without my smartphone."

"My phone is my computer."

"My company does not pay for my phone, so mostly use it only during personal time, or to contact family during work time if a parent is in the hospital or guests are arriving."

"The smartphone is a fantastic productivity tool. It allows me to significantly function no matter where I am in the world. The fact that I use the phone for personal and work issues is a benefit to the employer because I mix work and personal time together, thereby spending more time working than I would otherwise."

"I used to remember when there was a difference between working and NOT working ... lately it's just a change in location."

"With the constant connection I get a lot done, but there seems to be more to do as I get it done and I make the mistake to continue to use during meetings."

Whether executives use cell phones at work or companies sell shoes via smartphones, they can connect on mobile at any time. Mobile facilitates activity, from shopping to communicating with others at all times of the day or night. Most important, untethered consumers will expect information, products, and services to be available when *they* want them, no matter when that might be.

Mobile customers consume information differently from their mobile phones than they do from other media devices, and savvy marketers will adapt to participate in that altered content interaction. Video is one medium that will change in character to be consonant with mobile's strengths; as a marketing force, video will be more significant than many believe, which we discuss in the next chapter.

Customer Engagement in a World Gone Mobile

With the rise of the untethered consumer, the substantial growth and use of smartphones, and freedom from time and location limits being added to the mix, mobile marketing requires an approach different from that of earlier marketing methods. The concept is not about mobile marketing as much as it is about marketing in a world gone mobile.

Looking at the smartphone as just another sales or marketing channel misses the scope of the mobile revolution. Mobile is not incremental, it is transformational. It takes the concept of customer engagement to a new level, where the customer is totally in the driver's seat and each interaction is unique in the interplay between customer and business or brand.

The good news for marketers in a world gone mobile is that all businesses start at the same point. For a company to be effective and create customer engagement in a mobile environment, it must provide clear value. While that value in the short term may be a discount or coupon, mobile customers will ultimately expect more from the companies offering products and services to them.

Mobile Business Goal Alignment

The marketing strategy for interacting with the untethered consumer should align with the goals of the business, and should take advantage of the new opportunities presented by mobile capabilities. The first step in this process is to evaluate the current and future mobile use of current and future customers.

Different demographic groups can be associated with specific mobile phones or platforms, so the first step is to determine what your customers use, that is, the phones they own and the mobile platforms they use, such as Apple, Android, or BlackBerry. One way to determine customer use patterns is to conduct a survey that simply asks customers what kinds of phones they use and whether they have smartphones. Another approach is to launch a mobile website and track the difference in traffic compared with the regular website. It is likely that a percentage of any given audience will have smartphones; the question is whether that percentage represents a small or large slice of your particular customer group. It is also possible that the best customers of your business use one dominant category of phone, such as a smartphone. You should then research what your customers are actually doing with their mobile phones. Are they texting, e-mailing, comparison shopping, buying, or watching video? The types of actions they perform can provide an indication of the manner in which they might be most comfortable interacting.

As we speak with businesses regarding their mobile approach, a common thread is the company's initial instinct to create a mobile app. While this may ultimately be a logical approach, it is not always the best place to start, at least in the short term. Creating an app limits use to smartphones, and while a significant number of people own them, millions of others have non-smartphones.

This leads back to the initial question: Which type of phone do most of your customers use? For some businesses, especially well-known brands, it is *expected* that at a minimum they will have a great and useful smartphone app, and many do.

Over time, the majority of the market will migrate to smart-phones, depending on price consideration and various other factors.

And it is the smartphone that is driving the mobile revolution. This is because of the value proposition of smartphones: the computing power and sophistication of smartphone technology can provide consumers with unique abilities to gather tailored information on location, helping make their lives better and easier. This improvement can relate to saving time and money, automating processes, or even helping to stay connected with loved ones through real-time video communications.

Follow Your Customers

Mobile phone use is evolving, as more features are introduced and more people learn about them. In fact, one of the challenges of the mobile industry is that businesses are still learning about the capabilities offered by various mobile companies. With so many established and start-up companies in the nascent mobile industry, it can be difficult for a business to get a handle on the current capabilities of mobile phones and on future possibilities.

Because individuals naturally are most familiar with the features and capabilities of their own personal cell phones, they can be tempted to view the market through that prism. Without appropriate research on the spectrum of mobile features available and on what their particular customers use, business leaders risk missing potential market opportunities.

As you'll see in cases throughout the book, many businesses have found exactly what their customers do with their phones, and they track in great detail specific customer–company mobile interactions. This is one of those times in history that customers are ahead of businesses. Because there are hundreds of thousands of different mobile applications and billions of people using cell phones, consumers are discovering and utilizing phone features and applications faster than businesses can keep up with them. As consumer behaviors evolve in tandem with emerging mobile capabilities, businesses that don't monitor and track these behaviors risk being left behind.

It is essential that businesses follow their customers' mobile use patterns and preferences. Otherwise, a business could end up creating a mobile product or service that doesn't match the behavioral characteristics of its own untethered customers.

Mobile Engagement

Marketing in a world gone mobile means turning the many-decades-old marketing concept of AIDA on its head. AIDA, which stands for Attention, Interest, Desire, and Action, describes the traditional stages of the selling process. Marketers must get the attention of the customer before they can hope to convince him of anything. Then they have to raise interest, typically by showing the benefits of the product they're offering. They next need to increase desire for the product by showing how the product can satisfy the customer's needs. The final step, the key step of getting the customer to take action, takes a bit more persuasion, essentially closing the deal.

Over the years, the concept has been modified to AIDAS, to include satisfaction, with companies focusing on customer satisfaction after the sale. In recent years, marketing has expanded to encompass what is known as the Voice of the Customer (with its own acronym: VOC), a process designed to determine customer needs and desires. This process involves gathering information on customers to better understand their needs, and may involve conducting focus groups, meeting with customers, observing consumer behaviors, and inviting customers to be involved in the product creation process.

In the AIDA model, the company or salesperson is directly and actively involved in driving the sales process with the customer. Seasoned salespeople watch for signs from customers that indicate how effective the sales pitch is; for example, they listen for specific questions customers may ask during the sales process. The company drives the traditional AIDA process. With mobile, it is different.

The untethered consumer may never give a salesperson a chance to use any of the AIDA process. That's because the consumer drives the process, which becomes faster and more intimate. The customer is using information from his mobile phone to assist him in the buying process. The difference with mobile is that the customer is interacting with something or someone at the other end of his mobile phone and any questions may be addressed to that contact through the phone. More good news for marketers is that with mobile, the ability to interact with a customer during the actual buying process increases, when marketers or salespeople realize that they can do it both on location and while on the other end of a mobile communication. Businesses need to realign to deal with the inbound, mobile customer who reaches out to a company for information or service rather than being sought out by the business itself. This is a customer either on location or at the moment of purchase who wants to interact immediately with the brand or business. She may want information or assistance based on her stage in the purchase cycle, or even based on her location at the business itself. At the retail level, this means training frontline sales associates to recognize a mobile shopper and equipping those salespeople to interact intelligently and effectively with this new breed of m-powered buyer. This is the new engagement model. It means taking into consideration the information the untethered consumer pulled to her phone from various sources in the process of making a purchase decision.

Find Solutions That Drive Engagement

The road leading to PepsiCo headquarters in Purchase, New York, is lined with stately mansions set back from the main drive. Just around the corner lies an extremely well-manicured garden of 168 acres known as the Donald M. Kendall Sculpture Garden. It's part of PepsiCo World Headquarters, named for the former Chairman of the Board and Chief Executive Officer, who commissioned the gardens that bear his name. Kendall had imagined an atmosphere of "stability, creativity, and experimentation" that would reflect his vision of the company.[48]

The sculpture collection was started in 1965 and comprises forty-five works by major twentieth-century artists. The PepsiCo headquarters, which comprises seven square blocks linked at the corners by towers, lies at the center of the garden. The building opened in 1970 on what used to be a polo field. In 1980, the gardens were extended, incorporating features relating the sculptures to their immediate surroundings.

Inside this building, many minds practice creativity and experimentation with mobile in a way that would no doubt have made Kendall proud. "Mobile is hugely important," says B. Bonin Bough, Director of Digital and Social Media at PepsiCo.[49] "It's the only device you have with you 24/7. Overnight, it became a place you can build apps."

PepsiCo does not get sidetracked by simply creating mobile apps, but rather takes a holistic approach to all things digital. "We're trying to look more at the portfolio; it's not enough to look at a text message or an app, we need a portfolio of apps," says Bough. "You need to find places where people want your brand. Mobile has become this whole new space platform in your product. How do we bring valuable utility through these devices?"

Bough and team act as an internal digital research and development department for the company, keeping a constant focus on customer engagement. "Our business is about building relationships and engagements," says Bough. "This is digital engagement." On his desk are reflections of all things concerned with the world of the third screen: three TV remotes, a PC and printer, a thumb drive, an iPhone, and an iPad, all within easy reach.

PepsiCo has been one of the most active large brands in mobile innovation. One example is a mobile loyalty program Bough's team designed in collaboration with PepsiCo Foodservice called Pepsi Loot. "The Foodservice people said they wanted to explore location-based opportunities," says Bough. "We said 'Why don't we reward our retail partners?'"

To do that, the company focused on creating a mobile app to show consumers where nearby Pepsi products were located. Once downloaded, the iPhone app uses the consumer's location to map nearby restaurants and other establishments that serve Pepsi products. The intent of the application is to create engaging experiences by linking the customer to locations of Pepsi products and inviting customer interactions on location.

Because of PepsiCo's active involvement in mobile, the team was already aware of developers who could create such an app. "We had a relationship with Zumobi, so we turned the Foodservice people over to them," says John Vail, Director of Interactive Marketing Group, Pepsi Cola Beverages.[50] The Zumobi Network publishes free smartphone applications supported by premium sponsorships. Zumobi uses a high-quality media advertising platform and counts among its clients Mercedes-Benz, Unilever, Southwest Airlines, Hewlett-Packard, and Best Buy.

The Pepsi Loot app first creates awareness and drives traffic to restaurants that serve Pepsi. As an incentive, customers on location (identified by the geolocation technology in the iPhone), can "check in" and receive points in the form of Pepsi "loot." After the first check-in and after every three subsequent check-ins, the customer has accrued enough Pepsi Loot to get a free digital song download from the online Pepsi Loot Store, which features more than 250,000 songs from a large catalogue of well-known artists.

With 285,000 employees and annual revenue of close to $60 billion, PepsiCo is the world's second-largest food and beverage business. A business that large and spread out is not a good candidate for a central-ized mobile strategy. The company is instead experimenting around the world, whether at the World Cup in South Africa or the Super Bowl in the U.S. "It's not about trying to overlay a gigantic grand strategy," says Bough. "We look at best practices. Innovation comes from everywhere. As a model, organizations don't know how to staff this stuff. You need to have cross-disciplines in the room."

"We try not to use our advantage as a negative," Bough says. "We have a lot more brands and customers than a lot of businesses. Our partners look to us and we try to bring them (vendors) new thinking. We look at how we can help, since we have loyalty experts in house."

Because of PepsiCo's sheer size and scope, the idea of digital inno-vation coming from almost anywhere seems part of the company's DNA. But rather than mobile companies approaching PepsiCo and trying to sell them on something, it's more likely that innovations arise from people at PepsiCo being on the lookout for opportunities and fresh ideas. Someone internally may say she wants to explore location-based marketing and the company ends up collaboratively creating Pepsi Loot, for example.

In another case, PepsiCo launched a marketing program with Stickybits, a New York start-up, by putting out a mobile app that allows anyone with a smartphone to scan a barcode and see unique messages associated with that code. Users can participate in challenges and fun contests by decoding the messages with their apps. It was PepsiCo that found Stickybits, not the other way around. "I happened to be at event where Stickybits was presenting in California," says Bough.

The key to PepsiCo's success with mobile is that it is willing to experiment. "We like to test things," says Vail, who started with the interactive group at PepsiCo in 1996. "In 2003, we all sat in a room and at the time SMS is what defined mobile." Pepsi launched its first mobile campaign the next year. The company's mobile efforts evolved from simple text messages, "instead of people walking around with bottle caps," to letting people vote by texting, to sophisticated mobile apps. "SMS today is like e-mail in the '80s," says Vail.

"We were early moving to digital solutions," says Vail. "We went from an SMS experience and continued to evolve." By 2007, Pepsi had entered into mobile video. At the time, Sprint was the official carrier of the National Football League. "We were in South Beach and they were doing mobile video," says Vail. "The first mobile ads were pre- and post-roll, for Sprint users who had the data plan. It was the first time we pushed out video as part of the plan. Whether it was SMS, iPhone, or Android, we were looking at what the consumer is doing and looking at early adoption and then tailoring our programs. The marketplace has moved so fast."

To support numerous mobile and digital efforts around the company, PepsiCo created a resource to assist. "We built a center of excellence here," says Vail. "The goal is to find solutions that will drive engagement, an experience." PepsiCo's focus on engagement extends outside mobile, most notably through its Pepsi Refresh Project, in which the company gives financial grants to worthwhile projects. Project ideas can be submitted by anyone, and the public votes on which ideas to fund. "We give marketing dollars away to causes," says Shiv Singh, Director of Digital, North America, at PepsiCo.[51] "We give away $1.3 million a month for a year and have received 120,000 ideas, fifty million votes, and four hundred ideas funded. When a consumer is activated to do something, he engages and shares."

To ensure that the company keeps up with digital innovation, PepsiCo created the PepsiCo 10, a process that encouraged employees to look outward, seeking ideas being driven by promising start-up companies. PepsiCo invited start-ups to submit an online application in one of four categories: mobile marketing; place-based and retail experiential marketing; social media; or digital video and gaming. The proposals were to be evaluated based on their ability to impact brands.

To be considered, start-ups had to be in technology less than two years, have raised up to $2 million, or have revenue of $250 thousand," says Digital and Social Media Director B. Bonin Bough. The company started with a field of five hundred applicants, narrowed it down to seventy, and then narrowed further until they had twenty finalists. Over the course of two days, those twenty companies presented their solutions at a summit at PepsiCo headquarters. Brand managers from Pepsi-Cola, Frito-Lay, Tropicana, Quaker Oats, and Gatorade, along with media agency partners, voted to select the PepsiCo 10.

PepsiCo then partnered with each of the ten emerging technology companies, helping them execute pilot programs with PepsiCo brands and matching them with mentors from top media and digital consultancies. Of the PepsiCo 10, five focus on using mobile. The PepsiCo 10 winners that leverage a world gone mobile are:

AisleBuyer. This mobile shopping platform aims to improve a shopper's in-store experience by using smartphone technology to unite the best features of the retailer's systems. The idea is to allow a customer to scan items in the store and then use mobile self-checkout.

MyCypher. A dynamic mobile platform, MyCypher allows artists worldwide to create new music in real time by turning every mobile phone into a microphone.

Zazu. A mobile alarm clock and calendar reminder, Zazu provides people with calendar details, e-mail, weather, and news verbally, allowing them to start the day with all the information they'll need.

Evil Genius Designs. This interactive technology company develops mobile games and entertainment for guests while they're waiting in lines, such as at amusement parks, conferences, and arenas.

MotiveCast. MotiveCast offers loyalty and rewards-based mobile gaming using augmented reality and location-based services (both of which are discussed later in this book) to allow brands to discover and engage with consumers in branded, fun, interactive game play.

There is little doubt that PepsiCo will continue to innovate in mobile, with Bough's approach setting the tone: "Step on the gas and don't let up." Part of the explanation for the success PepsiCo has with mobile is the company's willingness to try new things. "It's about creating room to fail," says Bough. "It's about test and grow. You need strategy and insights."

Many large and substantive brands such as PepsiCo are considering how to best support mobile efforts throughout their organizations, which in many cases are global enterprises. Creating a center of excellence to help identify or develop best practices is definitely one approach.

For example, Intel, a company with more than 75,000 employees around the world, finds innovation from any number of places within the organization. To address mobile, the company looks to digital enablement, basically creating a technical support function and infrastructure around mobile, to assist efforts throughout the company. A start was to create a cohesive mobile Web strategy.

"The mobile Web is about looking for one piece of information," says Matthew Roth, Senior Marketing Strategist, who oversees Intel's mobile strategy.[52] Intel's revised mobile website was launched in early 2011, and emphasizes serving customers on location who need a piece of information during the purchasing process. "The content on Intel. com is not on mobile," says Roth. The mobile Web can detect the location of the customer, so information can be tailored to that particular place. Just as PepsiCo does, Intel targets its mobile efforts toward better serving and engaging with customers in a world gone mobile.

Provide Value and a Call to Action

The most significant aspect of dealing with the untethered consumer is the idea of providing value. Commercials or advertising messages sent to cell phones will quickly be shut out by the customer. Instead, mobile marketers must determine what customers want and find of value. What does your product or service do *for them*, and how can you encapsulate that value in a mobile website or a branded app? Is there a logical brand extension that customers can use? Some well-known brands have launched effective brand extensions that provide services to customers. For example, Jeep created the app Tripcast, which allows a trip to be tracked and that information to be shared with friends, so they can monitor your location along a route. "This was a strategic new channel to develop relationships," says Lucas Frank, Brand Manager at Jeep. "Our core business is developing the world's best sports utility vehicle and this is another way they can explore that lifestyle."[53]

An application has to be of use to a customer; otherwise, he may download it once and barely use it, or he may never download it at all. Businesses may also need to provide different versions of the same utility, such The Weather Channel's different weather-tracking applications, which are tailored to the type of phone being used.

Mobile also provides the opportunity for the untethered consumer to do something: to act, to buy, to seek information, to interact. This is where a call to action comes in. After you've established that you have something of value to the customer, you've got to get her to take the next step and act based on her attraction to that value. How easy are you making it for the customer to act and react? How easy are you making it for her to shop? How easy are you making it for her to buy? What incentives are you including for her to act now? In mobile, including a call to action is key.

Hyperlocal Mobile

One of the challenges of mobile is that it represents the largest mass of customers found in any medium but is also what is known in the industry as *hyperlocal*, dealing with a specific geographic location. While there are billions of cell phones, patterns of use are different with each owner. Each phone is also being used very locally, to gather information relating to where the owner is physically at any given time.

This presents a dilemma for large companies that want to reach millions of customers with marketing messages, because with mobile, each customer may be doing something different at a different time and at a different location. Engaging these customers takes a lot of planning, and may involve large-scale marketing promotions with the mobile component tied to TV advertising.

The key to hyperlocal marketing is to take into consideration time and place. What is the mindset of the customer likely to be during the mobile interaction, and where is the physical location likely to be? We'll discuss this issue in greater detail when we cover location-based services.

GLOSSARY

bright shiny object syndrome. Tendency for a company to rush into the next cool-looking mobile innovation.

freemium model. A base application that provides certain functions for all customers, which is free. However, a premium version is also available to customers for a fee.

monetize. To convert into money. For example, Web marketers explore ways to convert website traffic into sources of revenue; mobile marketers are looking to do the same.

Test and Learn

Interacting with untethered consumers is a relatively new proposition, as the mobile technology that untied consumers from their stationary screens is fairly recent. Because of this fact, all companies of all sizes should take a *test-and-learn* approach. With the Web in the mid 1990s, the approach was called *launch and learn*, because there was no established base that could be tested.

Unlike the early days of the Web, there is a well-established base of mobile customers; nearly everyone has a cell phone. With mobile, however, the m-powered customer rather than the marketer decides how she wants to relate to a company. The best way to allow this decision-making process to occur is to try new things and get feedback from the customer. Rather than a drawn-out product creation process and major product launch event, mobile requires a test-and-learn approach, followed by a scaling up of what works.

At the beginning of its mobile marketing effort, Vocalpoint, a program of a Procter & Gamble division, took just such a *test-and-learn* approach. Vocalpoint assembled a research panel of about four hundred thousand women, which it uses to test new product attributes. It then creates marketing messaging based on the research results. The messages are specifically intended to be spread by word of mouth.

When Crest created a new toothpaste called Crest Weekly Clean, the Vocalpoint team surveyed its panel and found that there was a strong feeling among consumers that the results of everyday brushing did not compare to the deep-clean feeling of a professional cleaning at a dentist's office. They also found that having a salon facial was a unique experience understood almost exclusively by women.

Based on those two valuable pieces of feedback, the group created a brand message: "Crest Weekly Clean intensive cleaning paste gives you a smooth, clean feeling in between dental visits," a message it spread via word of mouth through its panel of women. That campaign proved to be the most effective part of the overall media advertising, three times more effective than other media in driving trial of the product.

There are significant expenses associated with testing large panels, including costs such as printing, direct mail, and product samples. "We would love to figure out how to engage our consumers via mobile, then we could go to a broader group," says Stephen Surman, Relationship Marketing Manager of Vocalpoint.[54] "As soon as mobile technology allows the consumer to provide feedback more easily, we expect to go that way."

Vocalpoint tested mobile for a project for Procter & Gamble Productions, a media production division that created, among other programs, made-for-TV movies in partnership with Walmart. Before a Friday night show, Vocalpoint sent mobile messages to those who had opted in. On the day of the show, Vocalpoint sent tune-in reminders and suggestions to invite friends and family to watch as well. "We were just trying to get our feet wet in mobile," says Surman. "We wanted to get a feel for mobile opt-in and feedback on mobile messaging. It was a learning experience for us to see how consumers reacted to mobile messaging."

Through its test-and-learn approach, Vocalpoint found that the feedback was neutral to positive. They followed up for feedback on the movie, and found that people had appreciated the reminder to watch the program.

As is common for P&G's divisions, Vocalpoint will continue to test and learn. "We are proceeding cautiously, we don't want to overstep our welcome," says Surman. "Our strategy with mobile is to provide experiences of value when and where the women want it."

Test, Learn, Evolve

The concept of test and learn is a great starting point for all aspects of mobile marketing; it's where you find out what works, what doesn't, and what your customers want. One of the early USPT applications was the iFood Assistant from Kraft. The app allowed customers to browse thousands of recipes, determine what to cook for dinner that night, and create shopping lists that could later be accessed from the phone.

The iFood Assistant app is a good example of how a company can provide true value to a customer through mobile. Though Kraft has a free app called iFood Assistant Lite, its customers tend to go for the paid version once they get a taste of the features and the value it provides them.

While the app was introduced relatively early in smartphone apps history, the process evolved through a test-and-learn approach. "There were three phases," says Howard Hunt, Vice President of New Business Development at The Hyperfactory, the mobile advertising agency based in Australia and New York that created the app for Kraft.[55] "The first phase was to focus on recipes and create reach, scale, and usage," Hunt says. The second was to add more mobile platforms, so the app was available on more smartphones. This phase added new sections, included budget recipes, enhanced shopping list features, improved the search and store locators, and generally expanded the number of features. The third phase included UPC bar code–scanning capabilities so that consumers could scan groceries in their pantry, or see what their friends are cooking, and even get coupons through an arrangement with Coupons.com

Kraft and The Hyperfactory tracked consumer response as they rolled out each phase, adapting the features of the app as they learned what their customers found useful or, conversely, didn't like. Because Kraft started with a test-and-learn approach, it was able to determine the features that appealed to its customers and grow the mobile business from there.

Avoid the Bright, Shiny Object Syndrome

As the mobile industry continues to innovate and as brands test and learn, it is sometimes difficult to distinguish the solid long-term strategies and developments from the exciting but ultimately ephemeral ones. In mobile, there are regular announcements about new things, ranging from advertising platforms to mobile payment capabilities.

An innovation is often referred to in the mobile industry as the next *bright, shiny object* because it attracts all the attention at the moment. Bright, shiny object syndrome can cause a marketer to lose focus on the company's ultimate objectives.

There may be a new mobile platform, for example, that has extraordinary capabilities. Or maybe the innovation of the moment is a new way to display video, or to interact one on one. The temptation may be to immediately divert resources to that particular new technology. The problem with following the bright, shiny object is that your customers may not be equipped or inclined to use such an innovation. Whenever you are tempted to jump on the next bright, shiny object in mobile, go back to the test-and-learn approach. Ask your customers for feedback, or implement the new technology in a limited way to see how it works before committing to a direction that may be ineffectual in reaching your customers.

The highly interactive and personal nature of the mobile phone is leading to the development of new formats for content, generating novel ways to both create and consume text and images, which we discuss in the next chapter.

There's an App for That: The New Broadcasting

CHAPTER 5

Unlike the Web, mobile is not about visiting and interacting at websites, though that is one of the activities of untethered consumers. Mobile is about tapping into technology-based platforms while on the go; it's about downloading and using specific, customized features that enhance the mobile consumer's productivity, performance, and even entertainment breaks while leveraging locations and time as never before.

Mobile Content and Context as King

The smartphone is inherently a content consumption device. It has many other attributes, of course, but content consumption is key, and material is consumed differently depending on the medium. In a movie theater, content in the form of a film is broadcast to the audience, who sits back and takes it all in. What the filmmakers produced is what is transmitted. The choice of content is made well before the broadcast, as the moviegoer selects the movie, pays for a ticket, and then watches the show. Radio content consumption is similar, with varying selections being broadcast and the consumer making his choice by selecting a channel. In both cases, the consumer makes a choice in advance and selects the content he desires, be it a certain movie or category of music or radio format, such as news, sports, or talk radio. Television is similar, though pay-per-view channels of course offer more specific choices of programs to watch.

In all of these cases, the consumer makes a selection from the available offerings and leans back to consume the content. But in many of these cases, the consumer is stationary. Part of the magic of Sony's Walkman, introduced in 1979, was that it not only made the music portable—portable radios had already done that—it also made it personal. Individuals could walk around privately listening to the music of their choice while being shielded from noises or distractions around them. Not only did Sony sell hundreds of millions of the music players, but in 2009, thirty years later, it was actually outselling Apple's iPod in Japan.

The mass migration to the Web in the mid-nineties turned much of the passive recipient model on its head. Now consumers could find content from almost anywhere at any time. They found what they wanted and consumed it when they wanted. But like previous media, for the most part they had to consume content while tethered to a device, such as the computer where they conducted the search. Anything could be printed to be read later in a different location, but it was still a relatively stationary mode of content consumption. Even so, the amount of available content increased exponentially.

Watching TV and Reading on a Phone

Every new medium tends to initially replicate some features from past media, and mobile is no exception. When audio capability became widespread, books were converted so that people could listen to *books on tape*. Same content, different delivery mechanism. A similar move is occurring with mobile, as both video and print media—including television shows, news, books, magazines, and promotional materials—are being converted for consumption on phones. The migration of video and text to mobile is one of the changes least disruptive to people's behavior because they are already conditioned to look at their phone screens for various reasons, such as regularly checking for e-mail, text messages, or the weather.

Consumers in many parts of the United States can watch regular TV shows in broadcast quality on their phones via FloTV, a service provided by AT&T for an additional monthly fee. Another service, from MobiTV, provides some free TV shows as well as many live shows, like a sporting event on ESPN, with various additional charges based on one-month, three-month, or six-month subscriptions. The shows typically are the same ones that can be watched on a normal or high-definition television, which is where the majority of TV viewing will occur, as you would expect. This is a typical progression from one medium to the next, but over time different video will be created to take advantage of the unique aspects of smartphones. For example, short-form video programming of quick episodes of a new show may be created, or mechanisms for live, mobile streams with an easy selection process to pick the one to watch at any given moment.

Text is going through a similar transformation. Using the phone screen to text, read, and send mail or to view Web pages all led to consumers who are accustomed to reading on a phone. And just as companies sprang up to convert printed books to audio books and newspapers to news websites, companies are appearing to convert printed materials so that they can be easily read on mobile phones.

Zmags Corporation was founded in 2006 in Denmark, though its headquarters are now in Boston, Massachusetts, with central functions such as product development and customer service in Copenhagen and sales offices in Canada, Great Britain, and Denmark. The original mission of the company was to publish an e-magazine, which included video, audio, and other forms of high-quality media. When the magazine came out, other publishers approached the company for help with their publications.

The company ultimately launched a digital publishing platform and Zmags Mobile, comprising technical tools and a method for companies and content creators to translate their printed materials for smartphones. "We do interactive magazines and catalogs to create interactive experiences," says Peter Velikin, Vice President of Marketing at Zmags.[56] "Readers can zoom in on the content and publishers can see content on as many platforms as possible, and then track and mine the data."

The mobile platform allows a content publisher to transfer its content to mobile phones and track who views what, how much time consumers spend on which content, and what parts of the content attract readers. One of the attractions for publishers was Zmags' page-flipping technology, which gave the mobile publications the same feel as the printed versions. In addition to traditional publishers, marketers who wanted their promotional and marketing materials available on smartphones were drawn to Zmags' platform.

Converting content so that it is easily consumable on smartphones is not just for publishers. Companies with marketing materials that are typically printed, such as promotional brochures and monthly reports, can convert them to be read on mobile phones, giving customers an easy way to interact with the content. New mobile content delivery processes such as those from Zmags allow marketers to fine-tune their future content, because they receive statistical reports on the specific material that is most and least read.

Over time, a business providing content over mobile can determine the material that is of most value to its customers, and can gauge the best time of day for consumers to receive that material. While some of this could be done on the web, smartphones add the insight of location. Mobile allows a business to see how their marketing materials are read, whether by someone on the go, in short spurts, or all at one time.

Transforming the Book Experience

Each new medium is generally adopted in two phases. In the first phase, traditions and practices of the previous medium are transferred to the new medium. For example, a local newspaper makes its online pages look the same as its print edition or a half-hour TV episode is posted online.

In the second phase of a medium's transformation, companies experiment with and exploit the characteristics of the new medium. They reinvent the way things are done, reinterpreting them for the new medium. A great example of such a transformation on the web is YouTube, which showcases millions of hours of user-generated video content on a platform that did not exist before the Internet.

ScrollMotion in New York is one of these second-phase organizations, and is dedicated to changing the way books are consumed in a world gone mobile. Since 2008, software developers at ScrollMotion have been devising ways to use smartphones to publish and consume books of all types.

E-book readers such as Amazon's Kindle and the Nook from Barnes & Noble render print content on easy-to-read screens that emulate the look of a printed page. The user buys and downloads a book or other reading material and can access it to read when she chooses.

ScrollMotion took a different approach by customizing the book content, integrating audio, video, and other features made possible by smartphones, and focusing on making the text and graphics an integral part of reading on a small screen by introducing a high degree of interactivity.

The company initially created content in the form of more than eleven thousand e-book applications for the iPhone, which were distributed by Apple's App Store. Through partnerships with more than seventy-five global companies that publish books, magazines, comic books, graphic novels, and textbooks, ScrollMotion created the Iceberg Reader, allowing the publishers to use a common platform that empowered readers. In addition to maintaining consistent pagination throughout the book, ScrollMotion included features such as adjustable text size, the ability to add notes, searchable text, copy and paste with the ability to e-mail the text or copy to Facebook, and multiple ways to navigate through the book, all on a smartphone.

Over time, ScrollMotion expanded its concept to make the content available across other smartphone platforms. "In the transformation from pages to pixels, we need to help publishers convert their content so it can be portable across as many platforms as possible," says Josh Koppel, cofounder of ScrollMotion.[57] "The content has to live across as many app stores as possible. It has to be portable on Nokia, Android devices, or the next platform that has not even been invented yet. The only way to do this is to embrace open standards like HTML5."

Like many mobile start-up companies we interviewed while researching this book, ScrollMotion had a business model that evolved over time, as it moved from converting traditional trade books into other opportunities. "The trade book business is not our focus now; Apple and Amazon really commoditized that business," says Koppel.

"We're focused on building content that can't be commoditized, like children's books, textbooks, and magazines."

When the company first started, the strategy was to rethink the ways books could be read on mobile phones. "Our challenge was to imagine all the different types of content for a small screen," says Koppel. "The iPhone represented the first real chance of creating something that could be better than paper."

Rather than simply copying the text from the printed version, the ScrollMotion books for smartphones can include multimedia, video, audio, slideshows with scalable photos, tables, graphs, 3D rotations, live quizzing, text- and Web-based searching, social networking sharing capabilities, advertising integration, subscription capabilities within the app, and analytics and usage tracking. It incorporates many more features than a traditionally published print book could.

For children's books, ScrollMotion created the capability for parents to record their own voices, so their child hears that as she pages through a book such as *Sesame Street* or *Curious George*. The child also can pinch zoom images and see visual chapter menus. The company focuses on the re-creation of books for the mobile medium. Says Koppel:

> The scary thing about progress is that sometimes it steamrolls over the things that we love. For example, records. The transformation from CD to MP3 steamrolled over the art of music packaging. For years, when you downloaded music on iTunes, all you got was a tiny pixilated jpeg of an album cover, but the great loss was the entire visual side of music, cover art, posters, lyrics, and liner notes. I am sure that this was not a conscious decision, but we lost that entire art form. I see our work as building platforms to save the print media types that will get overlooked in this transformation from pages to pixels, things like trading cards, comic books, activity books, and all of the other small print experiences that are in danger of going away.
>
> We're helping reinvent how books live in an academic environment. We created the first pilot program of iPad textbooks being used in California Public Schools with Houghton Mifflin Harcourt. This is where the print revolution is really happening. E-books are

going to hit the tipping point in public schools. It's all about economics. Why print, house, distribute, and destroy books? Give a kid a two-hundred-dollar tablet, fill it with dynamic content, videos, interactive quizzes, and digital learning tools, and then connect it to a back–end teacher tracking system that lets educators look at the entire class in aggregate—that is going to be the game changer for education in America.

Physical media is looking very old. Evolution is a fast process, it is not slow. Tower Records? Gone. Virgin Megastore? Gone. Physical locations that sell media are going away.

In my early days, I would go to the Virgin Megastore in Union Square, in New York City, to brainstorm, because it was one of the few places that you could go to and see the physical manifestations of a brand across multiple medias. I could see the book, the DVD, the CD, the tee shirt, the action figure, and how a brand could work across different formats.

As the Virgin Megastore was going out of business, with signs of "Everything must go" plastered over every surface, I would walk in with my camera and take pictures of what had been one of my favorite places in New York City. The last week it was open, they took the last of the books from downstairs and stacked them, all tattered and bruised on these great big shelves on the main floor. And as I looked at this picked-over merchandise, all sloppily shelved and falling in on itself, I thought "This is why books can't live in physical form anymore." Just the act of lugging them all up one flight, to be discounted before they are shipped off to be turned into mulch. This is why digital will win.

Physical books won't physically go away, there's a real case that high-end books and high-end publishing will be OK.

Read a book on a phone? Kids will. They will not know a world where they go buy a book. A small screen is a very intimate way to read. And you always have the choice because you have it with you all the time.

As to market acceptance of the ScrollMotion approach, millions of customers have downloaded the company's reader and hundreds of thousands have purchased the children's books. After *Esquire* was published with ScrollMotion, there were a hundred thousand paid downloads of the magazine within the first three months.

Publishers or marketers license the ScrollMotion platform annually and use the tools to create their version of their content for mobile, with much of the process now automated. "Publishers have to own the creative process," says Koppel. "We're a software company, and we are building tools that continue to let publishers own the creative process of making books."

The consumer shift from printed books to electronic books occurred faster than many had expected. For example, Amazon reported selling more e-books than hardcover books by the middle of 2010, with growth projected to continue. Meanwhile, Barnes & Noble was considering selling its chain of brick-and-mortar bookstores.

"The market moves so fast," says Koppel. "As a company, Scroll-Motion is focused on one of the major categories where there have been no major format transformations. Music publishing started by printing sheet music, then as recording technologies evolved there were records, cassettes, eight-tracks, CDs, and MP3. In movies, there was your home eight-millimeter, Beta, VHS, laser, DVD, Blu-ray Disc, and digital download. Print has never done that. It has always lived on paper. The new class of devices started by the iPhone offer the first new platform for printed media. The big issue is how the content lives and who owns it."

Mobile has the potential to transform everything it touches. With USPT, marketers have the opportunity to totally rethink how to best utilize the new capabilities to better serve customers.

GLOSSARY

OVP. Online video platforms, typically provided by companies in the mobile industry and made available for those who want to distribute their video content.

pre-roll. Online marketing videos that people have to view for fifteen seconds or so before they can watch what they want to watch. You know some will try this on mobile.

RTB. Real-time bidding. The idea of bidding for advertising messages to appear on a mobile device based on time, location, or other attributes.

UGC. User-generated content, that is, content created by end users rather than by media companies. Can be highly valuable, because consumers may perceive it as more authentic and therefore more valuable.

Constant Content

A movie is like a full-course meal, surfing the Web is lunch, and mobile is snacking—constantly, constantly snacking. Mobile content consumption is continuous. There is no beginning, middle, or end. A movie has a start and a finish. A newspaper can be read front to back and you're done. A song plays from beginning to end. The Internet has some analogy to mobile in that millions of pieces of information are only a click away, but unlike mobile, a person ultimately leaves the computer. And with mobile screens, unlike with Web pages, there is less room for information other than the material the untethered consumer is trying to view.

Some businesses have observed this need for the delivery of relevant content to mobile consumers and created technological solutions to fulfill that need. Some companies providing such mobile solutions may have started with Web-based applications, but followed the market wave to mobile.

Outbrain, one such company, was founded in 2006 to help people find new and relevant content to read online and to serve publishers by distributing their content more widely. The company is headquartered in New York, and has its research and development office in Netanya, Israel.

Outbrain built technologies that predict the content a person will like; the company then presents a link to that content, similar to the way other online retailers suggest certain products to customers while they shop.

Many are familiar with the recommendation engine of Amazon. com, which suggests a book by comparing what you previously bought to the purchases of others who bought the same book; the engine locates other books these readers purchased that you have not. The company uses predictive modeling technology to predict the behavior or purchase pattern of a person based on comparing that individual's past purchases or behaviors to those of perhaps millions of others who showed similar behavior or made similar purchases. Movie rental company Netflix uses similar methods to recommend movies that quite accurately predict a movie you will like based on what you've watched in the past.

Outbrain's CEO and founder, Yaron Galai, says, "We want to offer readers the most interesting content links."[58] The problem Galai saw was that good content might be created, but either was not widely distributed or was not distributed to the people who would most appreciate it. "Publishers wanted to get their content links to readers outside their traditional audience," says Galai.

The idea for Outbrain came from Galai's own personal experience reading online. "I love reading blogs," says Galai, "I love reading newspapers. On the Web it drove me nuts that I had to sort through so much information. I had to find out for myself that a particular article was not interesting to me. I thought, There has to be a better way." Galai had worked at two previous companies that developed apps, so he was familiar with the overall process. One of those companies dealt with advertising. "The ads we served were ones that, as a reader, I would never want to click on," he says, "but when I read *Wired* magazine, I actually like a lot of the ads there. I thought there had to be a way to offer a reader content that was interesting and relevant."

Outbrain built a database of tens of millions of articles by using technology that constantly "crawls," or searches, content sites on the Web. Outbrain then creates simple Web links to these stories, and the links are automatically inserted at the end of an article on a subscribing publisher's mobile site. "The currency we use is a simple link," he says. When a person clicks on the link, she is brought to the article on the site on which it was published.

In addition to the tens of millions of articles that Outbrain catalogues, there are stories or pieces of content that are sponsored links, paid for by the subscribing publishers looking to attract more readers to their content. There are typically no advertisements or marketing messages with these links and usually none on the mobile pages that show the links, which appear at the ends of stories. If a person watches a video, he may receive a link to a relevant video at the end of the one he just watched. Depending on the content the person viewed, the link could be a sponsored link from one of the paying publishers or it could be one from among the tens of millions of links gleaned from searching the Web.

Many traditional publishers saw the value of extending their content reach, and Outbrain's client list reflects that. Media companies including *USA Today*, *Slate*, the *Chicago Tribune*, *National Geographic*, *The Seattle Times*, Golf.com, and the Discovery Channel use the service. The algorithms Outbrain created provide the most relevant story links, whether sponsored or not. "With mobile, in many cases the readers find the paid links to be the most interesting," says Galai. "It's more of a service to the reader, while traditional ads are more of an interruption. On the Web there are a lot of options on the screen but on mobile the content is so stripped of everything. Content consumption will increase on mobile devices because they're naturally geared toward consumption rather than creation. People are going to be consuming a large amount of content on mobile, which may be bigger than the Web in the end game."

One of the challenges of the mobile revolution is that, as with other transitions to new media, a marketplace typically takes what it has used in the previous marketplace and tries to convert it for the new medium. During the Internet revolution, for example, early Web ads were typically converted from traditional print advertising. The good news is that, over time, marketers take advantage of the inherent capabilities of the new medium, an evolution that will happen with mobile as well.

In many ways, this market dynamic played to Outbrain's advantage in mobile. "The publishers asked us to integrate the service into their mobile sites," says Galai, "because, unlike traditional Web ads that don't port well to a mobile screen, our paid links are just that—a simple hyperlink that can be delivered on any screen that can display a link."

The advantage to the publisher is increased consumer traffic to its website, for which it typically sells advertising based on the number of people who view that page, and presumably the ad, during a given time. One of the traditional measurement metrics in advertising is called CPM, or cost per thousand, which ties payment to the number of people who view the page or ad. One of the results of using Outbrain is an increase in website traffic, and therefore revenues, for the publisher.

The Role of Video in Mobile: The Reinvention Paradigm

One might have thought that television would put movie theaters out of business. The reality is that the two coexisted nicely, even though movies are shown on both media. And after watching movies on large theater screens, who would have thought anyone would want to watch them on the relatively small screen of a TV? Well, people did. And over time, TV programming evolved to take advantage of the medium: it featured sitcoms, drama series, on-demand shows, and yes, even movies that had concluded their theater run. The attraction of watching a movie on the small screen? You could see it in the comfort of your own home. And when Web use exploded, how many predicted that people would want to watch videos on a computer screen? It turns out that in one month alone in 2010, U.S. Internet users watched 34 billion videos.[59]

In each medium, visual content evolved into something new to take advantage of the strengths of the medium. For television, programming grew to encompass everything from half-hour sitcoms to sporting events to reality shows; it included news, entertainment specials, documentaries, and sometimes live coverage of events.

Video on the Internet, too, evolved to fit the character of the medium, with content ranging from rebroadcast television shows to user-generated videos. In December 2005, YouTube officially launched, allowing videos to be uploaded and shown around the world via the Web. Just a year after its launch, the company was acquired by Google in a move that combined the forces of YouTube's powerful media platform with Google's passion for organizing information and creating new models for Web advertising. YouTube struck contract deals with many media companies, including CBS, BBC, and Sony Music Group, adding a breadth of traditional video content to the catalog of videos generated and uploaded by users.

While people could use their computer screens to simply watch movies, they began to do much more. They discovered innovative ways to use video technology, capitalizing on exciting new possibilities that existed with the Web.

Mobile is the next video platform. Like movie, television, and computer screens, smartphone screens will accommodate movies. This doesn't mean that movies are the ideal video format for a phone, but as we've discussed, transitions to a new medium typically start with imports from previous media. The InsightExpress Mobile Consumer Research tracking study found that those who watch video on their mobile phones are most frequently watching full-length television shows, clips of movies and TV shows, and music videos. They less frequently watch movie trailers and user-generated video, and they rarely watch full-length movies.

The research firm also found that while the majority of mobile video viewing is done at home, the office is also a popular place to watch. The most common times to watch mobile video at home are 7 P.M. to 10 P.M., followed by 11 P.M. to 5 A.M. At work, the most popular times that people find to watch mobile videos are 12 P.M. to 5 P.M., followed by 8 A.M. to 12 P.M.

It's important for marketers to know that those who watch video on mobile phones are not necessarily representative of the overall viewing audience. For example, almost half of smartphone owners who watch mobile video say they're watching video or programming that they wouldn't watch on TV.

As with other behavioral aspects of untethered consumers, mobile viewing is more active than passive. More than a quarter of smartphone owners say they're more likely to click on a mobile video than on nonvideo content, and 37 percent who watch mobile video search out mobile videos on their phones. Mobile is inherently a pull device, and offers an experience qualitatively different from being at the receiving end of a broadcast channel.

New Content for a New Medium

New video content will be originated for the new medium of mobile, just as new video content was created for each new medium before it. Users are beginning to watch video on mobile phones in more significant numbers, and research shows that those who watch mobile video are heavy consumers of video overall. For example, 86 percent of those who watch video on mobile are regular TV viewers, more than half watch free video sites on their computers, and 40 percent watch TV channels on computer.[60]

Even more significantly, mobile video viewing is changing behavior, replacing video viewing on other devices, a shift that has huge implications for those who create, transmit, and market using video. About three-fifths of smartphone owners who watch mobile video say it has replaced other video content, with 20 percent reporting that it is replacing TV for them. Just as there are people who watch TV shows on their PCs, there is a growing number of people who watch television programming and YouTube videos on their smartphones.

And while the use of social networking is significant on mobile devices, 15 percent also say mobile video is replacing free websites or social networking sites on computer. More than one in ten say watching video on mobile is replacing watching TV shows on computer, another indication of not only a behavior change but a potentially significant market disruptor, if more smartphone owners watch TV on their phones, with potentially different habits for commercials.

The sources of video on mobile are also somewhat varied; the largest percentage of viewers watch video from the mobile Web, and the next largest percentage watch via apps, closely followed by those who watch from both the mobile Web and apps. This means that marketers planning to advertise or market using mobile video need to determine which of the mechanisms—the mobile Web, apps, or a combination— is best for them.

In either case, TV-related content on mobile will be significant, since almost a third of smartphone owners who have apps have downloaded a TV network–related or TV program–related app on their phones.[61] Again, iPhone users are above the average; almost half of them have downloaded a TV-related app. The networks with the most commonly downloaded apps are ESPN and The Weather Channel. Those who have not downloaded TV apps say they lack interest either in the concept of TV-related apps overall or in the specific apps available.

Evaluating whether your customer base is interested in apps related to your company is both the challenge and the opportunity for marketers, as discerning mobile customers seek out the apps that provide personal value to them and dismiss others. If your company is considering developing an app, you will have to determine the best value an app can provide to your current or potential customers, or you risk wasting time and resources on the development process. American Airlines, for example, has produced an app that provides flight schedules and flight status, and that gives customers the ability to book flights, check frequent flyer account status, and check in. And American Express created an app that makes it easy for cardholders to check their current balance, review recent charges, and receive account alerts by text message.

Though using a TV-related app while watching a network broadcast is not yet common, many marketers and broadcasters are tracking that behavior closely to see how it evolves. There's potential, of course, to allow mobile consumers to interact live via their phones while watching. However, activities such as voting and entering contests are not high on the list of what untethered consumers currently do, according to research conducted by Knowledge Networks. Based on Knowledge Networks' data, the activities consumers perform most often using TV-related smartphone apps include:

Watch video clips	53%
Check TV schedule	41%
Download content to phone	38%
Listen to music	37%
Play a game	34%
Read articles about actors	31%
Watch entire episode	31%

Look for recipes/instructions	21%
Vote for a contestant	20%
Enter a contest	17%

Interestingly, of those who do watch video using TV-related apps, the majority watch on their smartphones in addition to their regular television viewing. Knowledge Networks also found indications that individuals with TV-related apps preferred to use the web for TV content, followed by an app, and in last place a mobile website.

Age of the Mobile Video Platforms

The dramatic increase in the amount of video available and the growing number of places video can be viewed have given rise to companies known as online video platforms (OVPs), some of which have sophisticated distribution networks. The era of the large, centralized network broadcasting video to anxiously waiting viewers planted in front of one main screen is fading.

Will people watch video on a phone screen in the future? The short answer is: absolutely. It just won't be traditional, feature-length movies, but rather new forms of video better suited to mobile. Of those consumers with TV-related apps, the majority watch video clips and about a third watch full episodes.[62] Other common activities are checking the program or network schedule, downloading content such as wallpapers and ringtones, and listening to music from a program.

Kyte, a privately held company headquartered in San Francisco with offices in New York, London, and Hamburg, was founded in 2006 and provides Internet video services for the web, connected televisions, and mobile platforms. The company's customers include some of the best-known names in media, including ABC, Clear Channel, ESPN, Fox News, MTV, and Universal Music Group. Kyte also serves corporate clients globally, including Nokia Germany, Swatch, Armani Exchange, and Monster Energy Drink.

Kyte anticipated the move to video across platforms based on its experience in the music industry, where it catered to recording artists, who were using the service to distribute music videos. "We started as a consumer service for people to share video with each other," says Gannon Hall, Chief Operating Officer of Kyte.[63] "It was analogous to the blogging explosion. Today all the major publishers have blogs. The same trend is happening in video. We started supporting high-definition video and professional video formats, which over time became more attractive to media companies. Media companies adopted the platform as a way to easily deliver live and on-demand video to audiences on the web, social networks, and mobile phones."

Kyte created a Web-based console so that a company could upload and manage video and playlists, create and manage video channels, and manage user-generated video content. It also created analytical tools to track video production, distribution, and viewership. The company's technical framework facilitates the fast and easy creation and transfer of video applications for iPhone, Android, BlackBerry, and Nokia. The Kyte platform allowed a company to essentially create a video and instantly make it available via all its outlets, including its website, Facebook page, Twitter account, and, most important, all mobile phone platforms. Says Hall:

> The impact of mobile is really profound. It's not just about mobile devices. This has introduced a new computing model. First you had full-feature phones, then BlackBerry, and then the iPhone and iTunes App Store, which fundamentally changed the whole nature of mobile computing and it disintermediated carriers from the content distribution game.
>
> It also introduced a touch- and gesture-based human interface, which is fundamentally changing how people interact with computers. The mobile practices being adopted today represent where all of this is going. There's a convergence of mobile technology, media, and overall computer technology.
>
> TVs are becoming Internet-connected devices as well, with startups like Roku and Boxes releasing "over the top" Internet-connected

set-top devices and the big guys like Apple and Google putting their full muscle behind TV products of their own.

Kyte is all about how to deliver media to audiences on different devices at different times. We're about distributing media over Internet technology, following the movement to all media being delivered via Internet technologies. At the end of the day, it's about making it easier to deliver content, including video to a phone. It all has to do with content.

For example, on an iPhone certain content is perfect, like while you're waiting for your car to be washed. Short-form video is great for that. However, for larger devices longer content is better for a lean-back experience. I'm not sure linear television (e.g., an episode of *Lost*) is the right form for mobile.

Different devices are contextual. If you're connected to a TV, the context should be different than mobile, so there has to be tailoring for platforms. Take mobile video advertising, for instance. It started with thirty-second spots, then went to fifteen, and now new, interactive ad formats are emerging.

Early in TV, radio scripts were read in front of a camera. Eventually, TV producers realized you could do more with the technology and created new content specifically for TV audiences. Mobile is no different, and publishers are just now starting to create content specifically for a mobile audience.

One example of new uses for mobile platforms was developed after the Haiti earthquake. MTV wanted to help, so the cable network had Kyte develop its Hope for Haiti iPhone app. MTV then broadcast "Hope for Haiti Now," a two-hour TV telethon to raise money for relief efforts. Viewers with mobile phones could download the app from the iTunes app store, watch the telecast live, and make real-time donations from their phones. The app was created in less than a day.

International furniture store chain IKEA used the Kyte platform to feature authentic video content on a special website devoted to a promotional tour in Germany that visited twenty-two IKEA stores in twelve days. The retailer broadcast live and uploaded raw content shot at the stores from mobile phones to the Kyte channel.

Online video platforms facilitate the distribution of mobile content on an instant and global basis. Marketers can use these platforms not only to reach their customers where they are at any given moment, but also to connect with potential new customers, as mobile video distribution grows ever wider.

Advertising on Mobile Video Platforms

It was only natural that, with the technological advances that sent video efficiently into the growing mobile world, marketers would begin to look for ways to get their video messaging into their customers' hands. With television, marketing was relatively easy: a commercial could be produced and then aired to millions of people. The downside was that, though millions at a time could be reached, there was no guarantee they would all be the right people. The decades-old and often-repeated advertising truism that "Half the money I spend on advertising is wasted, I just don't know which half,"[64] seemed appropriate for much of early television advertising. Monitoring of viewership is tracked as scientifically as it can be, considering the limits inherent in measuring a mass medium such as television. Mobile is at the other end of the spectrum. With mobile, each call-to-action can be monitored so that the effectiveness of marketing messages or advertising can be closely monitored, in real time. And in many cases, the action of a customer based on location can be monitored for effectiveness. Mobile, in fact, presents a challenge that is almost the opposite of television's: instead of viewing the single broadcast, the untethered consumer absorbs content from so many different places that it can be challenging to reach many of them when you want to. Part of this is due to market segmentation, but a significant aspect of it also is driven by the difference in technology.

In broadcast, for example, network executives and advertisers know in advance approximately how many people are likely to watch a particular show. Magazine and newspaper publishers also know in advance about how many people are likely to see any given issue, because media companies know their total circulation or audience size. Media planners and buyers have figured out over the years the combinations of media they should purchase for any given brand or marketer, as well as how to measure how many people saw the message.

For example, a company that wants its marketing message to reach sports enthusiasts could advertise in *Sports Illustrated*, on ESPN, and via other sports publications or channels. The advertisement or commercial would be produced and placed in the designated media. This strategy is relatively straightforward and well established; brands, advertisers, media buyers, and media companies all know how it works. Mobile turns that model on its head by adding the dimensions of time and location to the media consumption mix. With mobile, media buyers can target specific people based on where they are and on what they are likely doing. Whether their customers are at a football game, in a shopping mall, or at home in the evening, marketers can more easily gauge a customer's mindset based on the time of day and her specific location.

Untethered consumers still receive content from traditional media companies, as well as from a plethora of new information sources. The initial challenge for marketers has been how to reach mobile customers, how to reach a lot of them, and how to appeal to them. Compared with traditional media, mobile presents both challenges and opportunities for marketers and content providers:

- Consumers do not absorb content in the same way with mobile as with traditional media.
- Attention spans on mobile are shorter.
- The sheer number of mobile applications can cause market confusion, with many having similar capabilities, or people don't find them because they get lost in the pack.
- Innovators in mobile content keep raising the bar for content creation.
- Smartphones allow people to move quickly from screen to screen.
- An almost infinite number of untethered consumers can be reached at various times.
- Mobile facilitates extreme interactivity.
- Mobile allows immediate calls to action.
- Untethered consumers can be reached on location.

The dynamics of mobile dramatically alter the traditional advertising metrics of reach and frequency, that is, how many people receive a marketing message and how often. In a traditional print publication, reach and frequency are obvious. On the Web, it has also become relatively straightforward, because of technological platforms that help standardize the ways advertising is transmitted. For example, Pointroll, a subsidiary of Gannett Co., Inc., developed interactive and action-oriented online video advertising capabilities on the Web. Many Fortune 500 companies have used Pointroll's platform to transmit their video ads and track the views; in the aggregate, these ads have been seen hundreds of billions of times.

Where to Spend on Mobile Marketing

When it comes to advertising on mobile, the mantra is: "I know that all the money I spend on mobile advertising is useful; I just don't know where to spend it." With mobile, you can reach as many people as you want, where you want, when you want, but you can't reach them in the traditional way. The advertising will be different and the measurements will be different. Expectations and results will be different.

Crisp Wireless is headquartered on the twentieth floor of an unassuming Eighth Avenue building a few blocks from Madison Square Garden in New York City. Inside these offices, developers work on the technological mechanism that allows marketers to send sophisticated commercial messages to millions of customers on their mobile phones based on their location and to track who acted on those messages.

The company started in 2006, and focused initially on creating mobile sites for businesses, mostly in the media industry. Two years later, Crisp Wireless changed direction and began creating a common technology platform that allows publishers to more easily accept advanced types of mobile advertising. The platform also gives advertisers the ability to create highly engaging ads and more easily reach large numbers of customers across multiple publishers on that platform. "At the end of 2009, we launched the platform and changed the focus to advertising and changed our customer base," says Boris

Fridman, Chief Executive Officer of Crisp Wireless.[65] "With mobile, the publishers had to be able to accept the ads and there are very few suppliers of this type of technology since there is a wide range of platforms. It was an easy sell for the publishers." Crisp Wireless signed more than seven hundred publishers and media companies, including CBS, The Wall Street Journal, *Esquire*, *Bloomberg Business Week*, *Good Housekeeping*, Lifetime, *Fast Company*, Hearst, and TBS, among others.

Crisp Wireless created various mobile advertising formats for the publishers, and then worked with the publishers to enable and certify them to use any combination of formats. The ad formats for mobile phones include:

- Full screen, which takes up the entire phone screen
- Expandable, which start small but allow the recipient to enlarge them
- Location-based, determined by the geographical location of the phone (once the user agrees to be tracked); can direct the mobile user to the nearest dealer or retailer of a product
- Tap-to-video, an ad component that leads directly to a video when the screen is tapped or touched
- Tap-to-social network, an ad component that leads directly to a social network such as Facebook or Twitter when the screen is tapped or touched
- Commerce-enabled, which allows the user to buy instantly from a designated retailer, for example, from the iTunes store when using an iPhone.
- Tap-to-call, an ad component that provides a phone number for a user to tap or touch to immediately dial the number

The technology platform of Crisp Wireless allowed these advertising formats to run on a variety of mobile devices, so the advertisers or publishers don't have to customize for each type of mobile phone. This is one example of a platform being created to serve a new market need, that of creating smartphone-ready advertising rather than simply trying to repurpose content and approach from the web.

Many businesses and ad agencies are experimenting with different components of the Crisp Wireless platform, to see what works best for their customers. For example:

- To promote its Echo Zulu campaign, the U.S. Air Force created an animation ad on the home page of MTV's mobile site that included a graphic of a plane that appeared to crash through the screen of the phone. The "crash" was followed by an expandable ad that a user could tap to take him directly to a video. The target market was sixteen- to twenty-four-year-olds.
- A Lexus campaign for *Fast Company* involved a complete site sponsorship that allowed Lexus to promote its IS convertible to tech-savvy professionals via their iPhones. The *Fast Company* home page carried a banner that read "Brought to you by Lexus," and featured an ad that, when clicked or tapped, took the person directly to dealer locations.
- The American Museum of Natural History wanted to promote two specific exhibits, "Journey to the Stars" and "Lizards and Snakes," so it created auto-expanding ads that closed after three seconds, and included expandable banner ads and two tap-to-video banners. The museum targeted untethered consumers by running the ads on AccuWeather.com in New York City.
- Paramount Pictures used full-screen home page takeover ads on Fandango's iPhone-optimized site to promote the theatrical release of *G.I. Joe: the Rise of the Cobra*. The ad was customized to run only once a day per person and clicked through to a fan quiz, which could be skipped in favor of continuing to the Fandango site. The campaign ran for two weeks prior to the film's release, and the company tracked high click-through rates.

These types of innovations will become commonplace, as companies begin to capitalize on the technological strengths of the mobile environment while better catering to the needs of the people migrating to those devices in ever larger numbers.

"Publishers see the growth of mobile," says Fridman. "Mobile for some publishers is now 30 to 40 percent of their traffic." Fridman, who wrote a book on wireless data for business in 2001, is enthusiastic about the potential for mobile. Referring to the difference in the technological development process for websites compared to smartphones, Fridman says, "Mobile is different. It's easier to go from mobile but tougher to go from online to mobile. The future of mobile is a virtuous circle. For advertising to be a business, you need audience. You need content for an audience. Advertising begets revenue and revenue begets more content. For commerce you need advertising."

Companies that have used the Crisp Wireless platform include Volkswagen, Ford, Sprint, Skittles, Intel, Coca-Cola, Estée Lauder, Lexus, Infiniti, and Toyota, among others. In addition to its array of ad formats, the Crisp Wireless platform has several other USPT features that global companies find appealing: "It has location information built into the platform," says Fridman. "But it asks for permission. Push-to-call is also built in."

One of the most significant aspects of USPT features is accountability. The promise of true one-to-one marketing, which has been getting closer to reality with each new medium, comes closest with mobile. The Crisp Wireless platform, for example, provides marketers with highly detailed data regarding responses to their ads, including:

· Number of seconds a person displays a home page
· Time of day each ad element is viewed
· Number of interactions with each ad
· Number of times a video is played
· Percentage of videos watched in their entirety
· Percentage of people who hit the tap-to-video banner

Each advertiser can learn in real time how any particular marketing message is being received. "Agencies can see how each of the ads performed on each site and then optimize for the next campaign," says Fridman. "Publishers are two-sided businesses. There's the consumer, reached with content, and marketers, who want to reach the consumers. This makes the market more transparent. In one aspect you can create gorgeous ads and on the other side you can distribute and then understand the behavior of the customer."

Using this type of technology and platform, you as a marketer can create and send a message to a very large group of potential mobile customers. You can then see what works, based on time and location. And you will be able to do this in real time, allowing you to modify messages on the fly based on current results.

Closed Mobile: There's a Map for That

The content and concept sources of apps are wide ranging: in some cases, mobile apps derive from functions and features previously in existence, though others are new to any medium. One of the best examples of a "borrowed" source is digital maps. These gained popularity through companies such as Garmin, the Kansas-based company that has been creating navigation and communication devices since 1989. Many car drivers have grown accustomed to those turn-by-turn directions, clearly spoken in the selected language, from devices either factory installed or rubber-cup-stuck to the windshield. Owners can download updated maps annually. The market need was apparent, so as soon as technical capabilities became available, companies such as Verizon and Google offered turn-by-turn directions via mobile phones. Granted, the screens may not be as large as those on some of the Garmin devices, but they are large enough and detailed enough to help drivers find their way from point A to point B, with varying options including fastest route, most scenic route, and so on.

A mobile map game changer occurred in April 2005, when Google added satellite views and directions to Google Maps, which had launched earlier that year. In February 2007, Google added traffic information to maps in more than thirty cities, and in June 2008 a new version of Google Maps, designed for mobile, added transit information for fifty cities around the world. The difference between traditional GPS tracking and mobile apps such as Google Maps is that the Google Maps app plots traffic conditions along a route and provides an estimated arrival time based on those traffic conditions. Even if the driver does not know about a traffic jam ahead, for instance, Google's app factors it into the ultimate arrival time.

But not all apps evolve from creations or services offered through earlier media. For example, on August 7, 2007, in Salt Lake City, Utah, Spot Inc. introduced the Spot Satellite Messenger, a product the company called the world's first global satellite tracker for consumers.[66] The Spot Satellite Messenger, a closed mobile device, was the first of its kind to use satellite messaging combined with GPS location technology, and was, at the time, quite advanced for a consumer product. The handheld device was about the size of a small walkie-talkie and used GPS satellite technology to determine a user's location without cell phone coverage. The unit initially sold for about $150 in the United States, with an additional annual ninety-nine-dollar subscription fee. Over time, the initial unit cost dropped to ninety-nine dollars.

The product was targeted at people who spend time outdoors, such as boaters, hikers, campers, pilots, and the like. With the push of a button, Spot can transmit a user's GPS location coordinates and send a message to an emergency call center or to friends, family, or coworkers to request help, track the user's location, or just let friends know all is okay. There were several preselected message settings that reached certain authorities; if you were boater, for example, and pressed the emergency button, the Coast Guard could be notified. The Spot services worked around the world, including in the entire continental United States, Canada, Mexico, Europe, and Australia, in portions of South America, Northern Africa, and Northeastern Asia, and over thousands of miles offshore of these areas.

On September 30, 2008, Spot Inc. received the prestigious 2008 Wall Street Journal Technology Innovation Award for its Spot Satellite Messenger. By the middle of 2010, Spot had initiated more than six hundred rescues in fifty-one countries on land and at sea.

Spot is a subsidiary of Globalstar, which was established in 1991 and began commercial service in 1999, and offers service from across more than 120 countries, as well as from most territorial waters and several mid-ocean regions. Using a low-earth-orbit (LEO) constellation of in-orbit satellites and a network of ground stations, Globalstar offers satellite voice and data communications services to government agencies, businesses, and other customers in more than 120 countries. The ground stations are operated by subsidiaries in North America,

France, Venezuela, Brazil, and Nicaragua, and in other locations by unaffiliated companies, or independent gateway operators.

This is an example of a dedicated, closed mobile device that, while not a phone, serves a distinct and sometimes unique purpose: sending a message or signal to notify others whether you are or are not in need of assistance, with your current location included. The key is that it works outside of normal cell phone range, such as several miles off-shore, beyond the reach of cell towers. There are some cases where this type of technology may be more effective than a smartphone, though it involves a relatively small percentage of the market. What services such as Spot show is that there will continue to be mobile devices outside of smartphones that serve distinct purposes.

Mobile Computers

There are handheld mobile devices that fall outside the area of smart-phones, which are sometimes referred to as apps phones, since they run applications. These other mobile devices enable two-way information flow between a company and any category of its workers, such as salespeople or delivery agents. These mobile devices typically are larger than consumer smartphones and allow varying functions, depending on the specific business use.

Foster Farms Dairy started in 1939 when Max and Verda Foster bought an eighty-acre farm south of Modesto in California's San Joaquin Valley. The operation began with a few chickens, but within a couple of years it included an all-Jersey cow dairy that distributed fresh milk in chilled bottles to the front doors of local residents. In the mid 1950s, the Fosters added a modern creamery, and a decade later they began pro-ducing cottage cheese, sour cream, yogurt, ice cream, and butter. Foster Farms Dairy has now grown into the largest privately owned dairy in California. Each week, Foster Farms Dairy milks more than five thousand cows at its five dairies located throughout Stanislaus County. The farm processes more than two million gallons of milk a week, milk that is distributed via eight additional facilities located throughout the state.

The farm has a team of delivery drivers who also act as salespeople at individual stores that buy milk and other dairy products from Foster

Farms Dairy. In the second half of 2010, Foster Farms Dairy equipped that staff with Motorola's MC 9500, essentially a heavy-duty mobile handheld device that allowed drivers to link wirelessly to the company's databases, providing the drivers with details of which products should go in which dairy cases. The farm then was able to manage and track inventory all the way from dispatch, to onsite delivery, through end-of-day reconciliation.

This is an example of a dedicated mobile device used for a specific need, in this case tracking products, inventory, and customer interactions. This type of device is often considered "industrial strength," even though it uses traditional wireless networks. This type of device would be more common within an organization for a specific purpose, such as Foster Farms Dairy's product and inventory control and tracking. These mobile devices are typically larger than smartphones—sometimes substantially larger—and though they may have touch screens and internal motion sensors, they are far from the category of smartphones, being dedicated to a specific purpose rather than able to run the unlimited number of features and applications of a traditional smartphone.

Using Apps Phones

On July 25, 2009, a seventeen-year-old Los Angeles high school student left her home to run an errand. She later called each of her parents to ask them how to withdraw cash using her credit card at an ATM. Other than the unusual request, there was no indication that anything was wrong or that the girl was being coerced into making the calls. When the girl did not come home, her parents notified the police. The student's body was found early the next morning in the front passenger seat of her black Volvo. A convicted felon ultimately pleaded guilty to her murder and was sentenced to life in prison.

Shortly after the tragedy, a team of software developers dedicated themselves to helping prevent such crimes in the future. They wanted to create a mechanism that would increase security around an individual and enable that person to silently call for help when needed. The developers created Silent Bodyguard, a free iPhone app that, when activated, sends emergency e-mails to seven contacts every sixty seconds, and includes the person's location.

"We're looking at creating custom applications for schools, so they can monitor the communications," says Justin Leader, president of Los Angeles-based Fun At Work, developer of Silent Bodyguard. The app can be used by anyone, but one of its primary markets is those people with access to their own security service, such as college students, whose campus security team typically has a staffed central monitoring facility. For a nominal fee, emergency messages can be sent automatically to all the person's Twitter followers or to multiple cell phones, says Leader. A standard text message output might say: "Please help. My location is ...," followed by a link to a Google map identifying the person's location. Students can include their roommates' information, and Silent Bodyguard would notify them as well.

Ten thousand people have downloaded and activated Silent Bodyguard and it has been used three hundred thousand times, many of which are test messages to friends. "The e-mails go to people you trust and the best e-mails go to trusted friends," says Leader. In addition to college students, there are numerous other potential categories of users for the app, such as realtors who show a closed house while alone.

Silent Bodyguard is an example of a readily available application that anyone can quickly download to his phone and use immediately. Applications like this can be created by almost anyone who identifies a need and has the capability to either program or hire programmers to develop and launch the relevant applications.

The key to creating a successful app is to appeal to the untethered consumer in at least one of three ways:

- **Make life easier.** People today are busy, and many are overwhelmed by the amount they have to accomplish in the course of a day. Any app that eases some of the burden of daily activities by making a regular task simpler or more efficient wins. This could be as simple as helping a person create a shopping list or notifying him when a desired item is available based on his location at the time.

- **Make life cheaper.** Providing value in the form of discounts or special offers can be very appealing to the mobile customer, because deals can be highly relevant based on time and on the location of the individual. Allowing customers to use their mobile phones to find the best price for a particular item in surrounding stores or online provides the customer with genuine savings.
- **Make life fun.** With constant connectivity and the always-on nature of today's workplace, people appreciate a break. This respite from daily life can take the form a game app or a challenging puzzle. (One of many examples is the app Angry Birds, which has been downloaded more than fifty million times.)

Apps are limited only by creativity. There are hundreds of thousands of apps, some featured throughout this book. Following are a few examples.

Virtual Zippo Lighter. Perfect for concerts, this iPhone app provides different Zippo lighter designs that a person can select and write a message on. With a flip of the wrist the lighter opens, and with the flick of a finger across the flint wheel it lights, all with sound. Special custom designs are available for ninety-nine cents. This app has been downloaded more than ten million times.

Knocking Live Video. This application allows one person to enter a friend's username and tap on the name to "knock"; once the other person answers the knocking sound on her own phone, she can see what the first person's phone sees, in live video. This can be done while the two parties are on the phone, so one person can show the other what she's seeing live while they discuss it. The app requires 3G network speed, but it works between iPhones and Androids.

InterContinental Hotels Group. With this app, customers get the ability to find and book hotel rooms, check rates, click-to-call to reach the front desk, view or cancel reservations for all seven of the chain's brands (InterContinental, Hotel Indigo, Crowne Plaza, Holiday Inn, Holiday Inn Express, Staybridge Suites, and Candlewood Suites). The Priority Club Rewards app has been downloaded more than seventy thousand times; mobile is generating revenue of more than $2.5 million a month for InterContinental.

Key Ring. Key Ring lets customers enter numbers from frequent flyer accounts and other loyalty program information, as well as scan bar codes from supermarket cards or other loyalty cards; the app digitally stores the information for later use, allowing retailers to simply scan the bar codes from the screen.

ChaCha. This app uses AT&T voice recognition, allowing a person to ask any questions, such as the location of a restaurant or store by speaking; the options are presented via text message, with web links.

Brookstone. The app from the store with the same name features store locator capability based on current phone location, as well as easy shopping directly from the app. Many large retailers, such as Walmart, have apps with similar features.

Take Me to My Car. This app does basically what it says. When you park your car, you simply tap "Park" in the app, and it remembers the location. Later, when it's time to find your car, you tap "Get Directions," and walking directions and estimated time are provided.

NFL Game Center. The app of the National Football League provides news about each team, standings, and, most importantly, running scores and play-by-play descriptions in real time. A premium version provides additional features, such as one-touch access to your selected favorite team as soon as the team's game kicks off and audio highlights of big plays. ESPN has an app that provides a broader look by including information on each sports team based on market.

DirectTV. This helpful app allows you to program a home DVR remotely up to fourteen days in advance. On the road? No problem. The app shows what channels you receive. You can search for television shows, movies, or programs by time and date, select the room where the DVR is located, and set to record from your smartphone. Comcast subscribers can use a similar app from Comcast called Xfinity TV.

OnTheFly. This app from ITA Software lets you shop for airfares for trips anywhere in the world. It provides exact airfare calculations with quick sorts based on airlines, fares, and departure times, and offers one-tap ability to e-mail a selected itinerary. The apps TripIT Travel Organizer and Orbitz provide similar features.

iHeart Radio. This app plays radio stations live from around the country. The user can select by music or talk category, and can listen to home team sporting events while on the road. Another is Tunin. FM iCar Radio Lite for the iPhone.

AAA Discounts. This app shows discounts for AAA members based on their current location. The discount location can be sorted by category, listed by distance, and located on real-time maps. The app also provides turn-by-turn directions to the discount location selected. A sister app, AAA Roadside, offers locations of car rental agencies and auto repair shops and provides direct connection by text or phone to roadside assistance.

Dragon Dictation. This app transcribes (quite accurately) what is spoken and creates messages that can be posted to social networks such as Twitter or Facebook or sent as an e-mail. It accepts multiple languages, including English, French, and Italian.

iSpain Cities. This app provides a guide to major cities in Spain. It contains features found in many travel apps, including a currency converter, hotel information, nearby restaurants with directions and contact information, and lists of useful addresses.

The number of mobile apps is projected to swell past the hundreds of thousands already available. Some of this growth is driven by major brands, which find logical business reasons to create functional and relevant apps, and part of it is driven by the creativity of established and new developers who have great ideas for fun or useful apps. As part of their core fabric, a large number of these apps include location capabilities, an area we explore in the next chapter.

On Location, On Location, On Location: LBM

There are times the m-powered consumer is at a location and a company can provide value in the form of helpful information, even if the customer is not in a position to make an immediate purchase. Location-based capabilities built into smartphones allow companies to provide relevant information to a potential customer immediately or even lets the customer store multiple locations that he can access later. For example, a customer with a smartphone may "check in" to a location through an app that includes location-based tracking. If the customer agrees, his location can trigger marketing messages about relevant products or services based on that particular location, and which appear within a certain timeframe. Marketers can use this customer detail as background information, so that when a customer contacts a company, the company is already prepared to be of service. The company can automatically pull up stored information, such as the location of the customer in relation to a store or even in terms of proximity to real estate for sale.

Marketing in Place

We call this approach of using location information in advance of a customer contact *marketing in place*. The location information from the untethered consumer's phone is used to better equip a business with useful information even before the company is contacted by the customer, to make later company-customer interaction more efficient and effective.

As an example, ING Direct, the largest direct bank in the United States, looks to capture location information and use it to make interacting with customers easier for them, a good example of *marketing in place*. Location-based technology can identify the location of a potential customer in relation to a particular house for sale, since the location of the house for sale is already known. "For us, location is crucial," says JJ Beh, Mortgage Strategy and Planning Lead, ING Direct.[67] "With reach, you get recognition but when it comes to consideration or monetizing leads, targeting matters more. Getting in front of that consumer at the right time matters."

With the ING smartphone app, a person standing in front of a house she is considering purchasing automatically can notify ING of the property location, since the smartphone would transmit that location and it would be paired with the location information of the property for sale. The customer, with one tap, also could save that information to be used later. "This leads to all-around, advance conversations," says Beh. "When users want more information on the property they're looking at, the mobile application would pull the MLS data of that particular property and display it, and should the user decide to contact the real estate broker/agent, she clicks *call* the agent and the app sends the property listing data to the agent, courtesy of ING Direct," Beh says. "Here there is an opportunity for ING Direct to seed or improve lender-to-real estate broker relations."

"When users are interested in talking about mortgages, clicking 'call' gets you into ING Direct's call center, starting the conversation and skipping the basics, such as are you buying or refinancing, where are you looking, which we pick up as the user navigates the application. With more data in hand, the conversation is richer, as in 'Mr. Rogers, looks like you're looking at financing 5 Sunset Way, and your calculations show you're interested in X.'"

By using location information this way, the customer can contact a business and already be steps ahead of the game. Rather than having to start at the beginning with who they are and what property they're looking at, and starting to ask questions about a loan, for example, the conversation could start right at the detail level.

As more businesses market in place, more customers will come to expect such service, driving more businesses to market in place. M-powered customers will decide when and where they want to be served by companies in this way. When they want the service, they will set their phones to "find me" and will expect their location information to be used to provide them with added value.

Marketing in place can also involve automated information. For example, a customer could download an application that launches when within the immediate area of a certain business, and that business could then send service messages, such as deals of the day, product location information, or even store layout. Over time, the untethered consumer will come to expect such location-based services. And while some related location-based services will be created and provided by third-party developers, it will be in the interest of a brand to facilitate and maintain its own direct connection with its customers on location.

Brick and Mortar as Asset

In the early days of the Internet, companies with physical stores were challenged as it became easier and cheaper for a customer to buy online. Online businesses had no physical sales structures to contend with and thus none of the associated costs. The Amazons of the world helped reshape consumer behavior so that shopping and buying online became a way of life. Why travel to a physical store to pay ninety-five dollars for an item when you could buy it online for seventy-five dollars and have it shipped within a few days? The value proposition became clear to customers. Brick-and-mortar stores were a deficit. Such businesses responded over time, of course, and any significant business with a physical outlet also sold its inventory online, to keep up with online competitors.

Mobile is set to transform yet again the value of those physical locations, this time in their favor, for those who get it. M-powered customers will search for items in stores and use their phones to determine whether they're looking at the best deal. They'll be able to scan items and conduct easy, on-the-spot price comparisons.

This on-the-spot customer knowledge will change the way sales-people on location interact with customers. Mobile-savvy companies will retrain their salespeople to be aware of the information that can be gathered by mobile and arm them with tactics to serve customers who are using the third screen as a shopping aid. Salespeople will have to be empowered to match prices or risk losing the sale.

The businesses that do not understand the new dynamics created by mobile will lose customers and never even see why. If a shopper scans an item and finds that she can get it at a nearby store for 20 per-cent less, she is likely to go to that other location. The lost sale (and lost customer) will be invisible to the first store.

For example, walking through Sears late last year, I came across a couple looking at a Kitchen Aid mixer, which had a price of $199 prominently posted. The man pulled out his smartphone, read the barcode, and told his partner, "It's cheaper at Best Buy. Let's go." And they left Sears, presumably headed to Best Buy.

I launched a bar code reader app (in this case, ShopSavvy) and checked the price. Sure enough, it was available at Best Buy for $179, a $20 saving, or 10 percent. That may not seem like such a big deal for a brand the size of Sears, which has about 2,500 stores in the United States and Canada. But if you consider the magnitude of the power of people armed with smartphones and bar code readers, the impact can be profound. If only one person a day behaved like the couple I watched—that is, they scanned a $200 item and left the store to pur-chase it elsewhere—the overall gross revenue loss to Sears would be that $200. Possibly, this is no big deal.

However, if that lost sale occurred once a day in each of Sears' roughly 2,500 stores in the United States and Canada, that would be a loss of $500,000. Again, the amount is not significant in the scheme of Sears Holdings Corp.'s revenue of $44 billion. But if one person a day walked away from the store because of a better deal elsewhere in each of the 3,921 total stores of Sears Holdings, which include Sears and Kmart, that would add up to $784,200 in lost sales. If this happened each day of the twenty-eight shopping days before Christmas, the loss would add up to $21,957,600. Again, $22 million is not a significant part of $44 billion. But if this occurred almost every day, say for 360 days, just one smartphone-armed person per store could lead to a loss of about $282 million in gross revenue.

What if ten people a day used their smartphones to read the bar codes on a $200 product at each Sears and Kmart, and found it elsewhere for less, then left the store? The loss of that gross revenue annualized would be $2.8 billion. And what if a person is scanning and comparison shopping for more than one item? Will that shopper go back to the store that had the higher price? The point is, this will not be done by only one person per day. It will be done by thousands of people. Mobile will forever change retail.

But if handled with correct policies and practices in place, brick and mortar stores become an asset. The company has a valuable opportunity when the customer is there in its store, and businesses will need to learn how to capitalize on that opportunity in the new world of m-commerce. Some of the questions companies need to consider in order to prepare for m-powered customers are:

- How will salespeople be trained to recognize m-shoppers?
- What is the policy for price-matching when a customer shows a brick-and-mortar competitor's deal on his mobile phone?
- What is the policy for matching prices when a customer shows an online competitor's deal on his phone?
- What information is shown when product bar codes are scanned by mobile phones in the store?

There are additional training practices that retail sales organizations can implement to satisfy customers even further. For example, salespeople could be taught to show customers with smartphones how the store's app (if it has one) makes the shopping experience easier. They could also show smartphone customers how to do price comparisons via mobile. Because many untethered consumers are using location-based services, regular and highly active customers can be identified, as we discuss in greater detail later. The advantage of linking mobile with brick-and-mortar operations is that a company can finally know that a particular customer is in the store, and can see the factors she is considering closest to the moment of purchase.

In Motion Research

With mobile marketing, it is not only the customer's precise location that can be useful but also his movements. Movement can help determine intent. For example, someone moving toward an airport is likely to be either taking a flight or picking up or meeting a traveler. Someone moving slowly and steadily down a street is likely to be walking rather than driving.

With mobile, there are ways to analyze a customers' movements further, using what I call *in motion research*. With in motion research, you can look at your customers' patterns of movement, including where they go and what they likely do; that information helps you determine how to best serve them. "Think of location in a different way and use location as a research tool," says Phuc Truong, Managing Director of U.S. Mobile Marketing for Mobext, a mobile marketing agency that is part of the Havas Digital group of agencies.[68] "It can be a lens of how the average person lives their life."

Mobext has offices in the Americas and Europe, and specializes in mobile marketing for brands including Sears, Amtrak, McDonald's, Volvo, Nike, Coca-Cola, BBC, and Dell. The company partnered with Locately, a consumer location analytics firm born out of MIT, to determine the movement patterns of untethered consumers in the course of a day.

As any researcher knows, asking questions in a survey provides what may be the person's best recollection of past events. For example, a survey that asks people how many hours or minutes they watched television the night before may provide answers that are not exact. This is not because the respondents lie, necessarily, but rather because they may honestly believe they watched TV for two hours when it was really closer to three, or vice versa.

Many companies use what are known as survey-based panels, which comprise a group of people who are intended to represent a certain category. Very rarely do panels represent the total universe of people. (A notable exception is Knowledge Networks, which has recruited a panel of more than fifty thousand people that is representative of the U.S. population as a whole. For such representative panels, the results can be projected across the population.)

In a typical survey-based panel, customers may be asked how many times a week they ate at a particular restaurant or how often they shopped at a certain department store. By using the actual motion and location of these customers' mobile phones, researchers or marketer can compare all the movements and determine actual movement patterns of untethered consumers with their recollections of their activities. While the recollections of any given group of people may not be totally accurate, the actual recorded movements of people with smartphones would be. Mobext recruited Sprint cell phone subscribers in Boston, Chicago, and New York, who agreed to share the GPS data from their phone every ten minutes over the course of two weeks. Participation was voluntary, with no incentives. The consumers did not have to do anything except agree, since the location information was automatically gathered via the Sprint network, once they opted in.

Over the course of two weeks, Mobext measured movements of hundreds of untethered consumers at locations including airports, hotels, train stations, national retailers, and supermarkets. "We tracked and accessed the device six times an hour," says Truong. "We took lat[itude] and long[itude] and plotted against a retail map." One of the intents behind the research was to help marketers determine the accuracy of their traditional surveys. This approach allowed Truong and his team to determine patterns of movement for the untethered consumers.

"Marketers talk about delivering the right message at the right time at the right place," says Truong. "Survey-based panels are just based on surveys. With location panels you could disprove or reinforce the results. For example, McDonald's does consumer panels all the time to determine how many times you went to a QSR (quick-service restaurant). If they do location panels, you would know how many times they go to other stores. This is a new field."

Research using location and movement of mobile devices can provide marketers with additional insights and context about their customers' behaviors. Following are some of the findings of the Mobext study:[69]

- Those who preferred Dunkin' Donuts were 33 percent more likely to dine out than those who preferred Starbucks.
- Those who shopped at Walmart were 60 percent more likely to dine out compared with Target customers.
- Of Target customers who dined out, about 25 percent went to a restaurant before going to Target, while 25 percent went to a restaurant afterward.
- The average frequency of fitness activities for those who went to quick-service coffee or doughnut locations was 50 percent higher than those who did not visit those types of locations.
- Visitors to Whole Foods were twice as likely to engage in fitness-related activities compared with those who shopped elsewhere.
- Half of those who visited Whole Foods also went to other grocery stores.
- Sears shoppers did not visit any other department store, but those who visited department stores other than Sears split their visits between multiple national department store chains.
- Half of Starbucks customers visited Dunkin' Donuts locations. But if an individual visited Dunkin' Donuts, there was a 67 percent chance he would visit Starbucks.
- Commute times were 20 percent longer for participants who lived in or near Chicago than for those who lived in or near New York.

Keeping Up with Customers

The marketing implications for using in motion research are enormous. Brands can use the data to see where and when their customers shop, by day, time, and location. They can use such research to see correlations between activities and then market to customers based on those relationships.

For example, if a restaurant determines that customers within a certain geographic area tend to work late on Tuesdays and Thursdays and tend to stop at a competitive restaurant after work, it could create special deals for those two days. If this same restaurant sees that its customers visit a particular gym or health club regularly, it could create a comarketing campaign with the club to reinforce both services to current customers as well as attract new ones.

Companies can also use such in motion research to determine where they can more effectively open new stores or where they may wish to close some. The research can be used to determine the right days and times for promotions and the incentives needed to keep customers loyal.

In motion research is not a continuous program but rather features periodic, short-term studies to determine traffic and movement patterns of certain current or potential customers. This can help companies decide how, when, and where they should reach out to these mobile consumers. "All consumers are using mobile," says Mobext's Truong. "It's the time of day, day of the week, and context that is needed. What is the mindset and what is the need at the time? The savvy clients get it. The phone can be used as a guide as we live our lives."

In motion research is one of the innovations spawned by mobile, yet one more aspect of the opportunities derived from location-based marketing. As the mobile industry continues to advance and the untethered consumer uses more mobile features, brands and marketers will be challenged to keep up; the risk if they do not is that they will lose customers to others who are leveraging mobile better than they are.

Driving, Keeping, and Converting Customers

As mobile customers use their networks to get information to make purchasing decisions and come to expect on-the-spot deals and discounts, marketers will have to become adept at influencing these untethered customers where they are, while they shop. Location-based marketing involves attracting the customer to the desired location, serving him by providing value while he's there, and making his experience worthwhile and rewarding. There are mobile technologies and companies that can support marketers for each of these aspects of location-based marketing. Outside of mobile social networking, the three distinct categories in location-based marketing are what I call *location drivers*, *location magnets*, and *location activators*.

- **Location Drivers.** These involve creating incentives to attract a customer to a location, and may include coupons or discounts. These may be regular offers or one-time events. Many different mobile technology providers are location drivers.
- **Location Magnets.** Location magnets offer value once a customer arrives at a location. This may be in the form of helpful information provided in, around, and throughout the particular venue, which persuades the customer to spend more time there.
- **Location Activators.** These involve the interaction with the mobile customer at the moment of purchase. When a customer decides to purchase or is in the process of actively buying a product or service, the marketer inserts additional value, such as an at-the-moment discount or a coupon to encourage a future visit.

At the moment and at the location customers are shopping, brands and marketers have the opportunity to reach out to untethered consumers with immediate information, service, and value. Strategies marketers might use include mobile commercial messages, video descriptions of products, information on products that can be scanned by customers using their mobile phones, and connections to other similar consumers.

The behavioral changes that are emerging because of the possibilities inherent in location-based information are profound and will evolve quickly as consumers adapt to scanning images and receiving on-the-spot information and value. Marketers and brands will have the opportunity to insert themselves at this moment and on location, even at times providing the mobile platform for consumers to self-aggregate. Using the phone as a payment mechanism will evolve and companies will move to *location-based selling*.

GLOSSARY

LBS. Stands for location-based service. Services provided based on the location of the phone.

LBM. Location-based marketing, that is marketing to the mobile customer based on the location of the phone, and presumably the customer.

LOCATION DRIVERS

ATTRACTING CUSTOMERS TO THE STORE

Coupons are big business. In one year, consumer packaged goods (CPG) marketers distributed a record-breaking 311 billion coupons, of which more than 3 billion were redeemed.[70] For consumers overall, this translated to savings of $3.5 billion. And shoppers aren't using coupons just for weekly groceries. Even though the most frequently sent coupons are for breakfast foods, of the top twenty categories sent, fourteen are nonfood categories. The most frequently sent coupon categories, in order, are:

- Breakfast foods
- Oral hygiene
- Pet foods
- Household cleaners
- Vitamins and supplements
- Paper and plastic products
- Hair care
- Candy and gum
- Fresheners and deodorizers
- Light bulbs, electric goods, and batteries
- Personal cleansing and bath products
- Detergents
- Skin care preparations
- Gastrointestinal remedies
- Cough and cold remedies
- Yogurt

- Packaged meat and seafood
- Laundry supplies
- Crackers, cookies, and snack bars
- Salty snacks

Coupons drive people to a destination, and businesses have used various customer incentives for decades to draw customers into their stores. Big box retailers use one-day sales, supermarkets use coupons printed in newspapers and sent via direct mail to attract shoppers, and many businesses heavily discount particular products as loss-leaders to attract large numbers of people with the expectation that they will buy more than the special offering.

Although coupons are redeemed in substantial volume, the problem with pre-mobile coupons is that they are more general in nature. For example, a supermarket sends coupons to people who live within a certain geographical radius of the store. Over time, marketers could determine approximate reaction for the number of coupons sent, because customers had to physically redeem the coupon, allowing the business to track the level of success.

But there was always a distance factor with traditional coupons. A store would be in a fixed location, sending coupons to a person also in a fixed location. The intent, of course, was to create enough of an incentive to get the customer to leave his fixed location to go to the marketer's fixed location. And to a large degree, the system worked. Until the web, it was the best businesses could do.

The web changed the dynamics of the system, allowing marketers to create coupons digitally so customers could search, select, and print what they wanted. By the middle of 2010, the Internet was the fastest-growing distribution channel for coupons.[71] Companies like Coupons.com grew in popularity, as people switched from cutting paper coupons from newspapers or circulars to searching online for the relevant categories and deals and printing the coupons for their next trek to the store. The company reported a 100 percent growth in one year, from $529 million to $1 billion worth of digital coupons printed or loaded onto their loyalty cards for later redemption.[72] In one month alone, digital coupons produced by the company totaled more than $110 million.

Digital coupons continue to grow, with almost fifty million people in the United States already using them.[73] But with these two systems, paper and the web, every coupon still had to be either cut out or printed and taken to the store.

Mobile marketing is now poised to transform the entire coupon value proposition. With mobile, the static nature of coupons is eliminated and customer location can be added into the equation. Rather than sending coupons to potential customers at their home addresses or allowing them to search online for coupons that must be printed, mobile allows marketers to reach out with coupon offers that relate to the merchandise, based on where the customer is at any given moment.

Like traditional coupons, mobile offers can still be used to draw customers to a store. If anyone doubts the potential effectiveness of mobile coupons, 20 percent of smartphone owners already say they've made a special trip to the store after receiving a mobile coupon.[74] Not only that, 45 percent want coupons sent to them by text message, 28 percent want to find them using an application, and 27 percent want to be able to text in to receive coupons while they're in a store. This is another example of an evolving mobile behavior that marketers will have to prepare for. If not, they may find their customers shopping at stores that are more adept at servicing untethered consumers.

The concept of matching customers to products in real time based on the customer's location has been around for well over a decade. Marketers have long envisioned a scenario in which a person driving by a particular fast-food chain, for example, could be sent an instant discount as she passes, prompting her to stop in. Two issues prevented this from becoming reality until now: the phone technology was not advanced enough to make it practical, and consumers were not yet ready to modify their behavior that dramatically.

Today, smartphones feature considerably more sophisticated technology, and these advances have spawned many companies dedicated to creating location-based capabilities that allow marketers to more easily reach customers. One of the key ways marketers are reaching out to these customers is with mobile coupons. And the strategy is working.

Research we conducted at the Center for Media Research at Media-Post Communications shows that the number-one mobile marketing category, based on return on investment (ROI), is coupons.[75] However, that same study shows that the mobile media categories that excite clients most are branded applications and mobile video, which come in well ahead of coupons.

The research does show, however, that 67 percent of those not yet doing mobile campaigns expect mobile ROI to come from coupons, while slightly more than a quarter see it coming from branded applications and exactly a fourth expect it to come from mobile video. So the majority of this group at least has the same ROI expectations of those who have had the experience with mobile. Both advertising agencies (67 percent) and their clients (64 percent) say they get the greatest ROI from mobile coupons. So while mobile coupons may not excite companies, they and their advertising agencies do, in fact, see and expect positive results from them.

COUPONS GO MOBILE

The leading digital coupon-reward business on the Web, Coupons.com expanded further by creating new ways for on-the-go consumers to use coupons. The company expanded into mobile by introducing two mobile applications, a Coupons.com app and one called Grocery iQ. They found that coupons accessed via mobile were similar to those accessed online. These are the most frequently accessed categories of coupons on mobile:

1. Ready-to-eat cereal
2. Yogurt
3. Refrigerated dough
4. Vegetables
5. Lunch meats
6. Dessert items
7. Portable snacks
8. Nutritional snacks
9. Cheese
10. Bottled water, noncarbonated

The Grocery iQ app, which has been downloaded more than a million times, has been positively received and rated best-in-class by multiple national newspapers as well as being featured in Apple's App Store and the Android Market. The app has also been featured on national broadcast programs, in major consumer publications, and on blogs.

As in the Web version, the mobile version of Coupons.com allows users to select from the available coupons and, with one tap, electronically clip them for later redemption. The coupons then can be printed directly from the phone, if the phone is connected wirelessly to a printer, or they may be printed from a computer from the Web page. The app also allows mobile users to select coupons and load them to their supported grocery loyalty card, where savings are automatically deducted at checkout, without clipping or printing.

The approach Coupons.com uses is a classic example of USPT, that is, using smart phone technology to provide greater value to the mobile customer, giving them features unique to the smartphone. The company took its initial mobile Web content and dramatically increased its functionality by creating a smartphone app. "With mobile coupons, there are stepping stones," says Steve Horowitz, Chief Technology Officer of Coupons.com.[76] Before joining the company, Horowitz led the engineering team that developed the Android operating system at Google. "In the near term, there's an app on the customer's path to purchase," Horowitz says. Meaning that mobile apps are being used during a customer's purchase pattern, whether planning from home or shopping in a store.

The Grocery iQ app allows customers to create a shopping list by tapping on a master list and typing the first few letters of the product or brand name. Customers can also add items to their "Favorites" list with another tap. Untethered consumers can tap items from their list as they shop, and when they hit "Checkout," all items are automatically moved into a "History" location on the app. Those items not checked remain on the list for another day.

"They can use a digital list right on their mobile device," says Horowitz. "By creating their list on the mobile device and organizing it by category, we can let the user know about offers and coupons specific to the categories of products they are actually shopping for. Users can print the coupons, e-mail them, or add them directly to their store loyalty card. When they go shopping, these coupons will already be on their shopping list and they will be sure to get the right products and the best savings." Another example of USPT by Coupons.com is the app's ability to scan bar codes of items in a user's home that he wants added to his shopping list. A quick scan of a bar code identifies the product, including details of flavor, size, and so on, and automatically adds it to the list.

Horowitz also demonstrated the way some segments of the mobile world are going by showing how a smartphone could recognize a product and add it to a shopping list without ever seeing the bar code.[77] He showed, too, how voice recognition will play a role, so that a customer will be able to just speak whatever he wants to be entered as an item on his list.

The Grocery iQ app has other features as well. For example, if a person buys groceries at Safeway and household goods at Walmart, the app allows separate lists to be stored for each of those two retailers. Another feature allows store aisles to be customized, so that the shopper can select which aisles she prefers to visit in what order, and can rearrange aisles to match the layout of the store where she shops. The shopper can also eliminate aisles she never plans to use.

A key feature for families is that a user's list can be shared with another person, and the list is dynamically linked once the other party accepts the invitation to share a list. With the mobile apps and the GroceryIQ.com website, family members can easily share lists among multiple users on iPhone, iPad, Android, and the Web.

BEHAVIORAL CHANGE IN GROCERY SHOPPING

The mobile marketing program Coupons.com has created and launched is not about technology as much as it is about behavioral changes triggered by its app and other programs like it. The idea of keeping a shopping list on a phone is not entirely new: Kraft launched its iFood Assistant back in 2008.

Kraft's paid application contains thousands of recipes that can be searched and ingredients that can be compiled onto a shopping list. Directions to the nearest store are provided, and include a list of aisles that contain the recipe ingredients. Kraft's app also includes features borrowed from Coupons.com's Grocery iQ app. "Kraft is a great partner of ours and they approached us a while back about building some features from Grocery iQ into their iFood app, since they recognized that we clearly have the best-in-class shopping list application," says Horowitz. "In particular, they are using our couponing module as well as our list-building and integrated product database, lookup, and scan capabilities. We have been working closely with the Kraft team for a while to enable them to integrate this functionality and use our couponing technology in their application."

This is a case where mobile technological capabilities, USPT, are causing a change in customer behavior. The change is occurring because of the customer value provided. A customer who is able to quickly scan items in her cupboard or refrigerator, list items in her phone, keep a shopping history stored in an app, locate items in the store easily, remember "Favorites," and transfer coupon credits before checkout is going to find shopping—and life—easier. It's not about the technology, but rather about the benefit provided by the technology. The value it offers consumers is the reason more than a million people have downloaded the app. It is just one more mobile feature that can assist customers in their daily routines.

"Mobile should be part of a broader strategy," says Horowitz. "Companies need to engage consumers with apps. For us, it was all about providing alternatives beyond the newspapers. The CPG (consumer packaged goods) companies have been using coupons for decades, and they spend billions to get consumers to stores and they need to have redemption controls and also understand their financial liabilities. When we deploy that digitally, there is direct control, which is far more efficient."

There are challenges in deploying mobile technologies at retail, not the least of which are technological infrastructure issues as well as training the people who work in the stores, some of which have high employee turnover rates. "In the medium to long term [the challenge of mobile] will be basically about upgrading of the POS (point of sale) systems across all retail," says Horowitz. But even with upgrades in place, challenges will remain, including interaction during the checkout process. An example of this would be scanning a code or showing a message on a phone to a cashier at checkout, to receive a discount or be identified by reward number. If the phone is dropped when it's being passed between customer and sales associate, who is liable?

One technological advance on the horizon is called NFC, or Near Field Communication, where a person will simply wave his phone near a checkout device and the two devices will communicate. "We'll have NFC in time," says Horowitz. "It's all about identifying the customer at the point of sale. We need to be able to associate that unique customer ID with their coupons to apply to their shopping basket."

Though Coupons.com was not necessarily looking to experiment with it, the company also practiced *in motion research* with notable results. After analyzing coupons redeemed by iPhone and Android users, the company found some notable differences. While users of iPhones cashed in coupons for women's body wash, those using Android tended to cash in ones for men's body wash. When it came to dinner meats, while iPhone users were going for chicken, those with Androids were cashing in coupons for pork ribs. In terms of cleaning products, those with iPhones leaned toward multi-surface cleaners, those that can require a little elbow grease. Android users preferred more of a drop-and-go approach, cashing in coupons for continuous toilet bowl cleaner.

Owners of each of the competing smartphone platforms also seem to have different tastes in pets. While iPhone users were cashing in coupons for fish food, those with Androids were preparing to feed the birds. The differences between the two were not insignificant. For example, iPhone users cashed in twenty-six times more fish food coupons than those with Androids (and presumably fewer fish).

While iPhone owners were redeeming coupons for disposable diapers, their counterparts with Android phones were looking to take care of themselves, with two times more of them than iPhone users cashing in coupons for arthritis pain relief.

IPHONE VS ANDROID OWNERS' COUPON HABITS

Category	iPhone Top Coupons	Android Top Coupons
Body Wash	Women's body wash	Men's body wash
Vitamins	Children's multivitamins	Adult or teen multivitamins
Personal Care: Other	Baby products	Arthritis pain relief
Pet Food: Other	Fish food	Bird food
Baby Needs: Other	Disposable diapers	Disposable swim pants
Dinner Meats	Chicken	Pork ribs
Household Cleaners	Multi-surface cleaners	Continuous toilet bowl cleaner
Magazines	*Entertainment Weekly*	*National News Weekly*

COUPONS, COUPONS, COUPONS

Besides market leader Coupons.com, numerous other companies offer versions of mobile coupons for customers. Some attempt to aggregate customers around a certain deal (the offer is contingent upon a certain number of customers accepting it), while others create offers based on location or by category. If anyone has any remaining reservations about the value of mobile coupons, one look at the results of Chicago-based Groupon should dispel them.

Groupon is one of the ultimate location drivers, providing a deal or offer of the day based on the location of the untethered consumer. It aggregates buyers, and if a predetermined number of buyers agree to the deal of the day, it is executed. The marketer sells more and the customer gets a great deal, as long as the buying commitment is large enough. The aggregation of buyers is powerful in a market, especially when it can be matched to items or services for sale. It is the ultimate linking of demand to supply.

The company received more than $130 million in funding from a venture capital firm that had backed Facebook, giving Groupon a value of more than $1 billion. Near the end of 2010, the company turned down a reported $6 million acquisition from Google. Groupon also grew globally by acquisition, expanding into the United Kingdom, Ireland, Germany, France, the Netherlands, Spain, Italy, Switzerland, Austria, Poland, Finland, Denmark, Turkey, Sweden, Norway, and Belgium. It then bought additional coupon marketing companies, expanding the company even further, into Russia and Japan. For all of the companies acquired, the name was changed to Groupon but the local leadership remained intact.

The total expansion placed Groupon into more than three hundred markets in more than twenty-five countries, with more than forty million subscribers. The number of companies offering coupons to mobile customers continues to grow. Following are but a few examples.

MobiQpons. This service offers coupons based on distance from the customer, sorted by company name. Participating businesses include Target, Sears, JCPenney, and Best Buy, all of which offer discounts, such as twenty dollars off on select games. At the bottom of each coupon is a coupon code that the customer shows to the cashier at checkout to receive the discount.

Zip2save. The offers at Zip2save are categorized by subject, such as automotive, computers and electronics, entertainment, events, and food and drink. Consumers select a range from one to 100 miles from their current location, and they are instantly shown deals from local merchants, based on distance. Coupons have an expiration date, and the customer can either electronically "clip" the coupon for later use or instantly redeem by tapping "Redeem" and showing the phone screen at checkout.

Valpak. Valpak lists coupons by category, including auto, dining, leisure, beauty, and home, and sends them based on the person's location. Pictures of pushpins on local maps show where the deals are located, with details accompanying each marker. Coupons can be shown on the phone when placing an order.

LOCATION MAGNETS

LAND OF THE INDOOR MAPS

Many people grew up using printed maps to figure out how to get somewhere, or to figure out how to get out of somewhere if they were lost. These maps were usually stuffed into the car door pocket or jammed inside the glove box, to be pulled out only when necessary. While the maps may have been updated once a year, not every owner replaced them with such frequency. Maybe it was that next, long vacation drive that caused the owner to think about getting a new map, perhaps one picked up at a local gas station along the way. For a dedicated trip, an AAA member could request a series of maps, sent free in booklet form, with page after page detailing every road to take on the trip, together with distances and estimated travel times. It was as manual as you could get. This mapping approach may seem odd to those who grew up finding locations digitally by using a car-based GPS or Google Maps.

The web brought digital mapping of the external universe to life. Digitally plotting trips and viewing roads and buildings from satellites in relative real time became the new norm. But that mapping universe was all external, and included only what could be captured by a satellite or drawn or depicted, such as roads and streets.

Mobile takes mapping to a whole new level by going inside. Large venues such as convention centers, airports, shopping malls, and hotels will soon all be mapped internally so that untethered consumers have a virtual handheld guide to the path they want or need to take. What's nearby? Just tap or click to find out. Need food? Tap to learn how to get to the nearest restaurant. Hear of a sale? Tap to find how to get to that store from where you are. Which meeting is where? Just tap the phone screen.

Internal mapping is a great example of what I call a *location magnet*. Once customers are in the mall or shopping center, internal maps can keep them there longer. Internal maps help customers explore and discover areas, products, or services they may have otherwise missed. Marketers have a relatively captive audience of customers perfectly located and in a shopping mindset.

The implications of internal mapping can be transformational for marketers. The ability to specifically locate potential customers in direct relation to products or services at any given moment represents an epic shift in information flow. Offers could be tested, research on traffic patterns and mobile searches could provide greater insight into consumer behavior, and customers could show companies what they like and dislike based on their actions and interactions with the company via their mobile phones.

The challenge for technology companies is that mapping physical locations is difficult, for a number of reasons. Personal observation is often required to map a venue accurately. There are issues with changes, such as one store closing and being replaced by another. One solution is to allow untethered consumers to send correcting input back to the mapping platform provider, which benefits the company as well as the person who frequents any given location by making the information accurate and up to date.

The concept of internal venue mapping for mobile is relatively new, so you can expect some bumps along the way. However, the value to both the customer and marketer are high enough that the results will prevail over time. Several mobile start-up companies have already mapped hundreds of locations, and they continue to add more daily.

ON, IN, AND AT LOCATION

With internal mapping, marketers will be able to reach mobile customers closer to the moment of purchase than ever before. With tracking built into smartphones and into more and more applications, it will become natural for marketers to track movements of consumers as they shop and travel, as long as any given person allows it. To gain that permission, marketers will have to provide value that offers consumers a strong reason to consent. This value might come in the form of an offer to get a better deal on a purchase, a coupon for real-time or future use, or even additional information about the customer's surroundings. Point Inside in Seattle, Washington, is one location magnet service that has been effective in persuading customers to agree to being tracked.

The company, started in 2008, provides detailed interior maps of large venues such as airports, shopping centers, and hotels, and includes automatic pinpointing of the consumer's location when a GPS signal is available. So if a person arrives at, say, O'Hare Airport in Chicago and has a lengthy wait for a flight connection, he can use Point Inside to find restaurants, restrooms, and gates.

While a person doesn't necessarily need a smartphone app to find a restaurant in an airport, Point Inside provides interactive, searchable maps so people can use free-form text and directory listings or tap on the map to get more information. The maps can also be downloaded in advance, so that travelers can use them while on the plane to plan a stopover, which means the smartphone does not need a live wireless connection to find locations once in the airport.

As a *location magnet* company, Point Inside has developed maps of the insides of hundreds of shopping centers and malls throughout the United States, and bases much of its information on first-hand knowledge. "We use a validator to walk a particular mall or venue as well as a variety of other methods with the mapping team," says Brian Wilson, cofounder and Vice President of Marketing at Point Inside.[78]

Customers walking through a mall can locate specific stores by category or by their location in the mall. They can also determine their own locations relative to their destination and instantly see a store's hours of operation as well as a phone number they can tap to call. Shoppers can see events and promotions at participating retailers or within the mall while they shop, and merchants can automatically update their offers through the platform. Marketers can use the platform's self-service features to create their own marketing messages and offers for roaming customers.

Meijer, a Michigan-based retailer that operates 196 stores throughout Michigan, Ohio, Indiana, Illinois, and Kentucky, launched its Find-it mobile app with Point Inside so that shoppers can see the locations of more than a hundred thousand items in a retail supercenter using their smartphones. "The real benefit of the Point-Inside platform is the back-end tools and automated processes that make it easy and fast to make changes in product locations or store maps," says Wilson. "We can automatically update the precise locations of products in the environment in near real-time."

Of course, Point Inside and other location-based services depend on the availability of a GPS signal, which can be problematic depending on the actual building or building complex. The other location issue for these services is accuracy of position, because GPS positioning is not exact.

To keep location mapping information current, Point Inside aggregates input from a number of sources, ranging from the retailers themselves to people traveling through the locations. "In any mapping application, the challenge is keeping the data up to date," says Wilson. "In some of our malls, a marketing manager may tell us something has changed, we also get feedback through the app, and we're working to 'crowdsource' the information."

MARKETING ON THE INSIDE

Many of the mobile platforms being created in various categories include self-service components built specifically for marketers to use. One of the main reasons the industry is evolving toward this approach is the total mobile access of the customer. A traditional marketing or advertising message aimed at a customer walking through a mall has less relevance than an advertisement the customer sees when she walks into a specific store or stops in front of a particular window display.

The Point Inside platform includes such self-service elements. Its publishing platform allows advertisers to create an ad unit, which can include text and images. The marketer then schedules the days and times the ad should appear, together with the location. When a customer at a mall looks at her mobile screen, she may view the ad in a list or it may appear as a star on the map. When the customer selects the retailer associated with the star, a full-page ad appears on her phone screen.

The key point is that the ad is associated with a particular store's location. If a customer does not select the store, she does not see the ad. "We are currently the only mobile application that can associate a specific advertisement created by the retailer in a self-serve way, with a specific map location inside a venue," says Point Inside's Brian Wilson.

It's likely that other big box retailers, the very large general merchandise stores, ultimately will provide real-time inventory, including shelf locations, sales, and promotional data, just like Meijer does today, says Wilson. "We'll spatialize the data such that a consumer can either search for a product and view its exact location on the store map, or access in-store promotions to see where those products are located in the store."

Point Inside sees one of its value propositions to marketers as its ability to take relevant destination content and link it to customer locations in real time. This approach to dealing with untethered consumers can provide new value by increasing relevance and timeliness via mobile. "We'll be able to understand what the customer is searching for and, at the appropriate time and manner, display alternative or complementary products and their locations," says Wilson. "We'll be able to enable retailers and consumer packaged goods companies to cross-sell, up-sell, or provide trial incentives to customers while they're in the store shopping."

With interiors mapping for mobile, businesses will also be able to add convenience to the shopping experience. "Based on a person's shopping list or product search results, we'll be able to provide an optimized shopping route," says Wilson.

The ultimate goal for mobile companies such as Point Inside is to move from location magnet to location activator, to be involved at the actual transaction level. For example, if Point Inside eventually knew, via its location-based technology, when a person entered a particular store in a large mall, it could correlate phone activities, such as viewing a promotion, with actual real-world behavior, providing a potentially rich research picture.

To take that a step further, if the marketer knows the precise location of the customer plus the promotions the customer viewed, he can measure the resulting transactions. This could lead to what Point Inside refers to as a *cost per visit* model of advertising, where retailers would pay only when a customer takes a meaningful action based on the advertisement or promotion.

A unique feature in Point Inside's application is that if there's no cell or Wi-Fi service, the platform lets the person provide his position by highlighting a landmark he sees, and the system automatically adjusts to that setting.

INTERNAL POSITIONING PLATFORM

Another *location magnet* company, Micello, is several years old and based in Sunnyvale, California. While some of the internal mapping companies are focusing on attracting advertising or promotional revenue to go along with their maps, Micello is creating platform capabilities for other businesses to deploy.

Like some of the other indoor mapping companies, Micello has mapped the interiors of large facilities such as convention centers and malls across the United States. In Micello's program, the untethered consumer appears as a dot on the map, and the dot moves as the consumer walks through the mall or other venue. Stores are identified on the map, and by tapping on them the consumer can view a description, phone number, website address, option to show the location on the map, and directions from where he is currently located. With one tap, the customer can turn the tracking off or on.

Ankit Agarwal, founder and CEO of Micello, says, "Four years ago I saw that the world was going to change because of mobile and we made a bet that indoor positioning would come. We're very venue oriented. We can now do indoor mapping and they're more accurate than the mall directories on site."[79] Unlike some of the other internal mapping services, Micello links its internal maps with Google maps, so that the customer and potentially the marketer as well knows her precise location both inside and outside the mall. For example, the application includes a compass, so a customer walking in a mall can see what direction she is headed, which is also linked to Google maps. "Some of the others take the directory map and use that, so the end result is not really geodata," says Agarwal. "We have the geodata. But still the biggest challenge in indoor mapping is scalability."

Micello creates internal mapping using a combination of sources, ranging from Google Street View to see the doors into a mall, CAD/CAM (computer-aided design and computer-aided manufacturing) drawings supplied by the malls, store and mall websites, and pictures on location. "It's a ten- to twelve-step process to create the vector data," says Agarwal.

For Micello, Agarwal says that creating the internal mall maps was part of the process that allowed it to highlight the platform's capabilities. The company started with malls in California, since that is where it is based, and then expanded across the United States.

"We started with the retail environment with department stores first so we could showcase the technology, with the compass and personalizing the map," says Agarwal. "To do a map of an indoor retailer, it's very easy. But for us, we go one level deeper and we know the data exists somewhere. We wanted to create a people-friendly map. I want to be able to show you what are the aisles at Target. With the malls, we just wanted a demo to be able to show what we could do."

Rather than creating a product for consumers, Agarwal intended to create product for businesses to buy and let them deploy it for customers. The idea is to sell the platform to malls, for example, and have the mall operator or another party sell advertising to retailers based on the location of customers at any given time.

"We're Google Maps inside a building," says Agarwal. "People get it. They see the value of having an indoor map. We have the first indoor mapping platform (Go!Shopping) to go live in Singapore, run by SingTel, who sells the advertising content. They're selling location-based advertising. And the mall owners want to get in on the action, because they want to keep the maps up to date."

The Micello platform tracks not only location, but also the height of the phone, which can be matched to the levels inside a shopping mall. "We have height that we collect when we make the maps," says Agarwal. "If a customer is on, say, level four, the advertising content would just relate to level four. Ultimately, if a customer is standing in front of a window in one store, a targeted advertisement or offer from that store can be sent to the person."

Micello also is targeting large conference organizers, since the company could map the floor layout with locations of exhibits and exhibition content. "We want to power those types of companies," says Agarwal. "A bunch of companies just want the inside data. The maps are for companies to make money from advertising. We're a mapping platform."

MALL MAPS FOR ALL OCCASIONS

There are numerous mobile mall mapping applications available, and their features vary. For example, while one app might present only static maps showing the location of each store or a diagram of a mall's interior, another might show similar information dynamically linked to the location of the m-powered customer. There are also applications available for different countries and in various languages. Here are just a few examples of mall mapping applications.

FastMall. This application provides maps of the insides of shopping malls in more than twenty countries, including Australia, Argentina, Japan, the United States, Brazil, Norway, Chile, and Spain, among others. It offers coupons based on location, store reviews by other shoppers, and check-in capability. A nifty feature lets a customer quickly map where he parked and record a voice message with it. Shaking an iPhone with the app open highlights the locations of all the restrooms in the mall. Merchants can buy advertising messages.

Mall Maps Australia. This app features internal maps of more than forty malls in Australia, including information about area malls based on customer location, floor maps of malls by level, and directories with store contact information such as phone number and website address.

Go!Shopping (Singapore). Go!Shopping offers internal maps of malls throughout Singapore. It locates the customer by the floor he is on; promotional information is provided based on the customer's location. Malls can be searched for stores, and results provide contact information including phone number as well as the store location on the map. The service is provided by SingTel.

Mall Maps Mobile. With this app, consumers receive lists of malls across the United States with store directories, driving directions to the malls, and tap-to-dial phone numbers of stores in the mall. It provides either a list of stores with contact info or an inside diagram of the layout of the mall. It does not take into consideration the location of the customer.

LOCATION ACTIVATORS

MARKETER PAYBACK: TASK-BASED REWARDS

While the location drivers attract customers to a specific location and the location magnets keep them occupied while they're there, it's up to the *location activators* to interact with them during the actual buying process. One of the ways location activators do this is by tracking customers precisely and then linking them to specific products at a decisive moment. For example, when a person walks into a store he could be offered a deal based on the department he's shopping in or, ideally, when he's near certain products. Or he might be rewarded instantly when he makes a purchase, which is not a new concept. For many years, supermarkets have automatically provided coupons at checkout based on what products the customer purchased. So if a consumer just bought Pepsi, he may receive a coupon for a different PepsiCo product or for a competing product from Coke, in an attempt to influence purchase behavior.

It would be only a matter of time before a location activator platform was created, and it came in the form of an app called WeReward. Rather than using coupons, which fall under the category of location drivers, WeReward gives consumers points for their purchases; those points can be turned into cash. The marketer only pays when a purchase is made.

"We created a platform that provides value for the brand and the consumer using the platform," says Ted Murphy, founder and CEO of Orlando, Florida–based IZEA, the company that launched WeReward.[80] "The customer earns discounts in a fun and social way." To earn points, customers have to prove they purchased the product by sending a photo, which is then verified with GPS data and reviewed manually. For example, Domino's Pizza, the launch partner of WeReward, ran a promo that stated: "Take a picture of your Domino's pizza box. Make sure that we can see the receipt on the box. Mobile orders@Dominos.com." Once a customer takes and sends a photo of the product he purchased, the merchant can see the photo on an electronic dashboard provided by WeReward. Key for the marketer is that WeReward is a self-service platform, so the marketer controls the reward levels and verifies approval.

As a bonus, the marketer can take customers' photos and highlight them on the company website or use them in other promotional efforts. WeReward also created a self-service part of the platform reserved for advertising agencies, so that the agencies can run the programs on behalf of their clients.

For customers, each point has a value of one cent, and one purchase may earn 100 or more points, which are seen in advance on the smartphone. Also, offers are based on the consumer's location, so the offers are always within reach, sorted by distance or searchable by subject or category. With WeReward, there are no coupons, just credits for cash; once points accrue to a value of ten dollars, the reward is paid directly into the customer's PayPal account.

"A coupon isn't something you'd share with a friend, there sometimes can be a stigma to it, like handing over a coupon at a restaurant with friends," says Murphy. "But with mobile, they like to share those experiences. And the advertiser gets all of this tremendous data back, like did the customer have a good experience or a bad experience. And they can post the pictures."

Privacy settings are up to the consumer—the customer sending the photo can decide whether or not to share the photo, though a photo is required to verify the purchase. The customer also has the option of automatically sharing the photo over social media platforms, such as Foursquare, Facebook, and Twitter. "It's amazing to see the content coming back," says Murphy. "The consumers are having fun. We had ten thousand downloads in the first week of launch but we had ninety thousand in the last three weeks. We expect this to be a multimillion dollar business in the first year."

This location activator company provides customers with a way to accomplish tasks, which are all focused around products. The validation of the task also comes from the GPS data transmitted from the smartphone when the photo is taken and sent. The platform is totally performance based.

"The merchant can set its own price," says Murphy. "It's like a Google cost-per-click model. In the online world, a click to me is worth money. We're trying to do the same thing in the real world. For a marketer with a low-priced product, the reward may be 10 percent or fifty cents. But the purchase of tires, for example, might be worth thirty dollars for a customer to make a purchase."

For the marketer, the platform tracks the return on investment and WeReward takes a percentage of each transaction, on a sliding scale basis. According to Murphy, "The most effective thing we've seen is that when someone goes and shares an experience, the people mentioning their feeds will use the @location, like the store name. Our customers are sending the voice back to the brands, and the person managing social media at the brands is seeing them."

AUTOMATIC LOCATION-BASED CHECK-IN

Another company developing location activators is San Francisco–based Shopkick, which launched a smartphone app that can identify when a person walks into a store. Shopkick allows customers to automatically check in at specific stores without doing anything other than crossing the threshold. The company installs what it calls a Shopkick signal in a store, such as Best Buy or Macy's, and when a customer walks into the store with her smartphone the system is alerted so she can be offered special deals located throughout the store. The automatic check-in is powered by small speakers that emit inaudible sound at or near the entrance of the store.

This service has the potential to expand into shopping malls, with a major mall management already agreeing to launch the service in its malls across the United States. Once the untethered consumer signs up and enters a participating store, he receives credits called "Kickbucks" that he can cash in at the store. In the case of Best Buy, the store's intent is to link its point-of-sales system so that a customer could receive a reward by walking past a display or at a register when he is checking out.

Brands and Geolocation

While some mobile companies play the role of the location driver, location magnet, or location activator, there are others that can arm a brand with location-based capability for instances when a brand wants to control its own activities concerning location drivers, magnets, or activators. Founded in San Francisco in 2005, Placecast was built on the premise that location is the defining characteristic of mobile. Rather than launching its own location-based products to sell to consumers, it provides the technological engine for brands such as The North Face and Sonic to create and conduct their own location-based marketing.

Placecast built its technology with the intent of serving customers in potentially very large markets. "We were a tech start-up five years ago and we were hyper-focused on very scalable technology," says Alistair Goodman, Chief Executive Officer of Placecast.[81] "We have ten patents filed in the area of location data and content management and the platform can run in more than seventy countries."

Placecast uses what is called *geofencing*, which creates a virtual perimeter of any chosen range around any location. When someone comes inside that perimeter, she receives a text message on her phone, if she is participating in the program. A geofence could be a mile or more around a store or it could be fifty feet from the front door, whatever the business decides.

To determine the location of the customer's phone, Placecast uses the GPS signal, location data from the cell phone carrier, and triangulation of the phone's distance from a cell tower. This is done only once customers have opted in to the program.

As a facilitator of a location driver, Placecast can be used by a brand to provide offers that lead customers to a store. "It can be things like coupons or discount codes," says Goodman. "For every brand we run a mini panel of consumers. It can influence store placements and inventory."

But location-based marketing does not always have to involve discounts or coupons as drivers; instead, information can be the driver that enhances the brand. For example, The North Face, an outdoor gear company noted for not discounting its products, can provide other types of offers to enhance the value of its brand. "They could do a geofence around places that they think are important to their brand," says Goodman. "[The company] could offer a weather report at a ski resort or maybe a recommendation of a route to take. It is marketing as a service, a valuable service brought to them by the brand."

The key to using location-based platforms is always to provide value to the customer. Says Goodman:

> We've been surveying consumers about location, and 80 percent of them understand we're using their location and they see it as valuable. Part of our learning in years of running LBS has been that opt-in is preferred by consumers on mobile, and when the offers are relevant based on where they are and when they are there, customers see them as hugely valuable and there are low opt-out rates.
>
> Another issue is the issue of privacy. Our service is double opt-in and easy to opt out. We believe very strongly in opt-in. Geofencing is a way of bringing relevance based on place and time, which, in mobile, is actually highly predictive of consumer intent. We've learned you don't need the precision of a geofence set right in front of the store. Think of it more in terms of mindset: it's Saturday morning, you're headed out to a shopping area with your wallet and your phone and you are going to make a purchase. Putting a geofence around a shopping area is an opportunity for the brand to be in front of you when you're going to make a purchase. Or buy within two or three days of the offer, with that place as a memory trigger.
>
> With mobile, where you are in the physical world is the most predictive characteristic of what you're planning to do. If it is Madison Square Garden it is the same venue, but a completely different audience profile and mindset from night to night. It could be a Celine Dion concert or a Knicks game—these are two very different places.
>
> The first issue we had to solve was the many different location data points and sources that refer to a place, linking the data to a single reference point on a map. The second piece is the ability to attach content to a location. Places in the physical world are changing all the time and twenty thousand businesses will open, close, or move every month, so location data is an issue. These pieces are required to do at scale since a universal database of places is never going to happen.
>
> We attach content to places, like hours of operation, user reviews, tweets, check-ins, and coupons. The map that pops up has

more information, including content a business puts in about itself. The company using the platform can publish that information back to a consumer when they're at a location and businesses can have sponsored icons on a map.

If you're a QSR (quick-service restaurant) like Sonic and you want to send an offer to consumers near the store and tailor it for the time of day and location, and change it four times a day to promote different menu items and each different discount code—this is the unique opportunity with location-based programs. The key of location and mobile is the opportunity to make offers available to consumers. The platform manages all the offers and maps.

Part of the challenge is the last mile and measuring the redemption of coupons or discount offers. Everything you do around the cash register in a retailer can be a huge barrier. Retail is slowly improving POS [point of sale] systems, but they are all different. Anything with POS can be challenging.

In addition to acting as a location driver, the Placecast platform can also play a role as a location activator. As it manages the content that a business wants to send to its customers, the platform allows a company to create customized, location-based offers sent through what Placecast calls "ShopAlerts." These text messages from a marketer can be sent when a customer who has opted in comes within the designated geofenced area of a business.

In a pilot program with American Eagle Outfitters, Sonic, and REI, Placecast found that 79 percent of those who received ShopAlerts said it increased their likelihood to visit the store and 65 percent had made a purchase by the end of the program.

Many chief marketing officers and heads of marketing at brands are paying attention to these location activators because they can affect decisions closest to a customer transaction. Location-based platforms such as Placecast allow a marketer to send advertising messages at a specific time and location and to track and analyze their effectiveness. "We completely analyze the customer information in the database," says Goodman. "We're more of a retention tool in the CRM mechanism and another touch point with the consumer."

Placecast is also finding high acceptance of location-based marketing outside the United States, where the company works with telecommunication carriers. "They have millions of customers and want to do location-based offers," says Goodman. "The overseas market is much more mature than the United States; there is more acceptance from consumers. A company can just render it with SMS or MMS, which is ubiquitous and interoperable, there's no need to turn on an app, and the message is super relevant. You can use location and time to leverage all the good things you're already doing. The brands tend to promote it."

The Long Stretch of Location-Based Marketing

While marketers will need to service mobile customers on the customers' timeframe, as discussed earlier, they will also need to serve them based on their location. But "location" can mean something other than physical location, as there are different types of locations—geographical and psychographical. While geographical location refers simply to where a person is located physically, psychographical location includes the likely mindset of the customer at the time. This knowledge can help marketers determine the most relevant messages to send, based on the likely intent of a customer at any given moment and location.

The geographical location is the more obvious of the two, and is the focus of much mobile marketing development. The first instinct of businesses that are integrating mobile into their marketing efforts might be to focus all their energies on the physical location of customers who are closest to final purchase. While this is important and offers a great opportunity for interaction, it is not the only location that should draw attention.

Instead, there is another location to consider, and that is the place of the mobile customer in the purchase cycle. As mobile devices get more sophisticated, people are using them more frequently and earlier in the purchase cycle. More and more customers research items well before arriving at a store, as searching for relevant item information on the phone becomes easier.

Mobile interactions ultimately will occur at both ends of the purchase cycle, as well as at all steps in between. Focusing all marketing efforts at one end of the purchase cycle could result in businesses missing out on a significant part of the mobile dynamics.

Being aware of location drivers, location magnets, and location activators can help you monitor the purchase cycle of your mobile customers. And those m-powered consumers will be reaching out to you to learn what value you can offer them, which we'll discuss in the next chapter.

The Finding:
Search on Steroids

On a computer, looking for something is correctly labeled a search. On mobile, a more correct label would be *find*, and I call the next generation of mobile tools designed to locate necessary information *finders* rather than search engines.

With mobile, a simple search is not enough. Now, that is not to say that what search engines like Google and Bing do are simple; in reality the mechanics are quite complex, which makes their use seem simple. A research tool known as Wolfram Alpha that contains more than ten trillion pieces of data runs on supercomputers, yet is searchable by simple questioning.[82] The end game for searching is that all knowledge will be searchable in relative real time.

The New Mobile Search: The Finders

Looking for information on a computer is often quite different from looking for information on mobile. When people search on a computer, they have an idea of what they're looking for. A student may be searching for information for a school paper. A business executive could be researching a competitor's products. Someone might be looking at a Staples catalog to view the weekly sales items. In essence, the searches are what I call *premeditated searches*. In a premeditated search, the person has some inkling of what she's looking for based on what her needs are. These searches involve more general characteristics than those that are typically needed on mobile.

As we've seen with other transitions to mobile as a medium, there are usually first and second generations. The first generation simply takes the way searches are being done on computers and transfers the method to mobile. This means using search engines such as Google, Bing, and Yahoo to click through to various web pages, which come up as results of the search. It is only natural for the first generation search tools to rely initially on existing technologies imported from the previous medium. However, the imported methods fail to take full advantage of all the aspects of mobile.

Mobile is about *finding*, and it requires a new kind of search. On mobile it is not so much about *searching* as it is about *finding*. People on the go don't need to know all the available options everywhere, they typically need to know what's near them now. The second generation of mobile search—the *finders*—takes advantage of the capabilities of mobile phones to help focus the results:

- **Location.** Where is the untethered consumer at the moment of the search? This can be determined by GPS positioning. This information can be useful for finding information by taking into consideration the person's current location. Location-based finding can be a very powerful tool for yielding results that are highly relevant and immediately useful.
- **Movement.** In what direction is the consumer headed, or is he relatively stationary? An untethered consumer traveling at thirty-five miles an hour is likely in a moving vehicle, while someone moving at two miles an hour is likely walking.
- **Proximity.** How close is the untethered consumer to any given product or service? Is he in a mall or a specific store? Is she at the office? Over time, this information will be invaluable for marketers.
- **Time.** What day and what time of day is the finding being conducted? Interactions at different times might mean different things. Someone trying to find something in the middle of the day, say,

during lunchtime, could be different than someone trying to find something in the middle of the night, potentially more of an emergency situation.

- **Context.** What types of things is the person trying to locate? Is she looking for a product near her or a store that is open at the moment?
- **Intent.** What is it likely that the untethered consumer is trying to do, based on what he is trying to find? Is he at the research stage of a purchase decision? Or is he so close to the purchase decision that what he finds will determine whether he buys right there, right now?
- **Connectivity.** Once the consumer finds the desired object or service, how easily can she be connected to it? Can it be accomplished with an immediate phone call or e-mail?

GLOSSARY

2D bar code. Two-dimensional codes, which are square rather than rectangular, traditional UPC (bar codes)on products and read by computers or registers at checkout. The 2D codes are recognized by smartphones and link directly to the marketer's desired content, which can be sent to the phone in a number of ways, such as a website link or message.

QR Code. Quick Response Code, a two-dimensional bar code intended to be read at high speed. See also 2D bar codes.

short code. The special code, such as 50293 or Disney, that customers can use to address text messages to companies for certain promotions or other purposes. Short codes are leased starting at about $500 a month. Branded codes cost more.

augmented reality. Using a phone to view something in the real world and having that image *augmented* by additional information displayed on the phone screen. An example would be holding a phone up to a building and information about the building, such as year built and name, would be displayed as text on the smartphone screen.

Untethered consumers are looking for on-the-spot knowledge and have a greater sense of urgency than is typical with a traditional search. The major Web search companies will undoubtedly play a role in helping untethered consumers find things, especially those companies that specialize in particular categories. However, new mobile finding capabilities will ultimately be more useful and relevant to a person with a smartphone looking to do (or find) something based on their current time, location, and mindset.

The smartphone opens up many ways in addition to traditional searches to find what is most relevant at the moment, based on the untethered consumer's location. For example, what are others saying about a particular restaurant the smartphone owner is walking by, where are a person's friends at the moment, are they nearby, or who has a better price on a product being viewed at the moment? Although many of the services or applications have not reached mass scale, they are being downloaded by the millions and are bringing value to the mobile consumer. These applications provide untethered consumers with information in context and relevance, such as knowledge about places and things around them, even if they did not necessarily 'search' for them.

Following are just a few examples of some of the finders. It is essential for brands and marketers to not only be aware of these new finders, but to also determine strategy and tactics that take advantage of this new environment. On mobile, the high value will not necessarily be in buying search terms on traditional search engines, although that will be part of the mix. Instead, the best results will involve the company getting positioned to be found at any given moment based on what the untethered customer is doing, where he is doing it, and when he is doing it.

Yelp. Founded in 2004, Yelp is one of the best-known finding apps due to its more than eleven million reviews from people who have patronized local businesses. Yelp sells ads to local businesses and provides information on restaurants, banks, grocery stores, gas stations, and more, based on the locations of untethered consumers.

Aloqa. Aloqa is a mobile service that uses the consumer's current location to proactively and continually list on her phone places, events, movies, and other activities that likely will be of interest, based on her preset preferences. If requested by the consumer, Aloqa can send a range of notices, including when the customer is near a Starbucks, for example, or a coupon when she is near a certain store.

Urbanspoon. This service displays detailed listings of restaurants, many of them high end, and shows where tables are available, letting the mobile user make a reservation, all in real time.

Geodelic. Geodelic automatically aggregates locations and information based on distance, relevance, and interest. The app "learns" over time, based on what the mobile consumer selects. One tap on a restaurant icon, for example, provides information on the one that is closest and most likely to be appealing, based on previous selections. The restaurant contact information is included as well as mapping to the location.

Finding It When Needed

Though some of the companies that provide such finding services started on the web, they are all moving to mobile, because of its larger potential market and because the applications are most useful to a mobile consumer as he moves about in the world.

PhoneTell was launched in Palo Alto, California, in mid-2010. It is a mobile phone app designed to make finding people, products, and services a lot easier and faster, especially when a person is on the move. "It's about quick connections to whatever you're looking for," says Steve Larsen, cofounder of PhoneTell.[83] "While web search is for information, mobile search is for action."

The free application, which Larsen calls "the world's greatest phone book," initially launched on Android smartphones. It integrates its address book functionality with the native dialing function of the phone. The company took a somewhat different approach than other finding companies. Rather than making automatic suggestions based only on, say, location and personal preferences, PhoneTell aims to present the most precise and highly relevant results related to what a user is looking for.

"We use a complex set of algorithms that include time of day, location, and priority modeling measured not only on the mobile user's past dialing behavior, but the dialing behavior of others as well," says Larsen. "We connect a user's mobile address book with hundreds of millions of phone numbers in our cloud database," he says. "We begin with public databases, such as the white pages and Yellow Pages (same as what you get when you call 411) and add Yelp, Bing, and others."

In addition to those databased phone numbers, PhoneTell allows users to add links to their personal, cloud-based contact databases such as Gmail, LinkedIn, Facebook, Outlook, or Salesforce.com. The company also found and added collections of hard-to-find phone numbers, mobile numbers, and hard-to-find customer service numbers at eBay, Amazon, American Express, and many other companies. For business listings, it also gathered location information, hours of operation, website, e-mail, and maps.

Consumers can download the app directly from PhoneTell or from the Android Market, and PhoneTell installs its phonebook-on-steroids as part of the phone's dialer. Once a consumer enters what he is looking for, the results are prioritized and delivered, each complete with a click-to-call button. (PhoneTell receives revenue when consumers connect with businesses where the company has a relationship, either directly or through partnerships with companies such as AT&T Interactive.)

Consumers with PhoneTell don't need to know many details of what they're looking for, yet the service finds relevant products, services, or people. Because the PhoneTell database stores businesses' hours of operation, part of its calculation before providing results includes whether the businesses are open at that moment. Results, for instance, when searching for "pizza" shows not only the closest pizza places, but also only those that are still open at 8:30 P.M. when you do the search.

Because PhoneTell is integrated with the phone's call stream, it provides consumers with information in both directions, both on incoming calls and outgoing finding. When users search for a product or service, the results include dialing information, so the user is one click away from being connected by phone to that individual, business, or service.

PhoneTell's vast database of phone numbers allows it to leverage that information to provide an additional service on incoming calls. When a person receives a call, information on the incoming call includes the name, phone number, and location, all of which are displayed on the phone's screen, even if the caller is not in the consumer's contact list. Once the consumer sees who's calling, he can either decline or answer the call or use the PhoneTell feature that allows one-click SMS (text) responses in real time if he chooses not to answer it.

If the consumer is in a business meeting, for example, and sees that her spouse is calling, she can send an auto-message that says, "I'm in a meeting but will call as soon as I get out." If she sees that the call is from a vendor she does not know, she can send an automatic message such as "I can't take your call right now but please send me an e-mail and I'll respond."

This is an example of a company providing real value to untethered consumers. Search advertising swept past display advertising on the web because it was driven by user intent, relevant results, and easy click-through, and the same dynamic is true for mobile finders such as PhoneTell. Plumbers use Yellow Pages Advertising because people who look there have a plumbing problem that needs to be fixed immediately. Mobile users also want something now. A person searching the web for "rental cars" from home at 4 P.M. on a Saturday may be looking for deals. But a person searching "rental cars" from a mobile phone at 9 P.M. at O'Hare Airport very likely needs a car immediately. Because PhoneTell knows the need or the intent of the user, the proximity of products and services, and the readiness to do business (hours of operation), its app can produce the most relevant sales leads for merchants.

Marketers should be aware that as apps providing such services proliferate, their customers will increasingly be connecting with them, or their competitors, through the new finders.

Finding by Codes

Another way untethered consumers will find things will be through codes captured and translated by their smartphone cameras. This will be accomplished in two different ways: by pointing the camera phone at UPC bar codes or at a newer type of code, 2D bar codes. Over time, more phones will come to recognize codes easily, whether on packaging, in magazines, or on billboards. Once the phone recognizes, or reads, the code, the customer can be digitally routed to any location or experience you, the marketer, has dreamed up. It can be as simple as a web page with information about the product and competitive price comparisons to downloadable applications with multimedia and purchase capabilities built in.

On June 26, 1974, at a Marsh's Supermarket in Troy, Ohio, a ten-pack of Wrigley's Juicy Fruit gum was run through a handmade laser scanner, for a sale of sixty-seven cents.[84] That pack of gum marked the beginning of the UPC (Universal Product Code) bar code era, where these ubiquitous codes have helped track the sales of many billions of items and speed shoppers through checkouts.

While there's a role for these series of black bars and numbers in the mobile world, there's an even bigger potential role for a newer version, though it's not a replacement for the trusty old UPC bar code. While the UPC bar codes carry information and pricing related to one specific product, mobile transports that information to a new dimension. This new type of bar code is called a 2D bar code. While the traditional UPC bar code is one dimensional, that is, it is read from left to right or right to left, a 2D bar code is read in two dimensions, right to left and top to bottom. The codes are essentially square rather than rectangular like UPC bar codes. They also look better than UPC codes and can be less intrusive on product packaging.

As in any other new medium, there are various versions of 2D bar codes, with different characteristics and purposes. For example, anyone can search the web and find a site where he can create a free QR (Quick Response) Code that can link to his website, include a phone number to call, or perform a number of other functions. There are companies that will print these codes on shirts, put them on business cards, or basically let you do whatever you want with them.

Different types of 2D codes can look different from each other. A QR Code, for example, has to be printed larger than some other 2D codes in order to be readable by the average phone camera, which may be a consideration for a business intending to add 2D codes to millions of packages. Several different 2D bar code companies exist, and each has its own approach. Following are a few examples of various code readers:

Red Laser. This is a mobile scanner application that has been downloaded more than four million times. The application can be used with mobile phone cameras that don't auto-focus. When a customer scans a product bar code in the United States or United Kingdom, the system searches for low online prices as well as prices from other retailers, with automatic search localization to find prices of products that are close by. The company was acquired by eBay.

ShopSavvy. ShopSavvy is an app from a company named Big in Japan (though it's located in Dallas, Texas) that has been downloaded more than ten million times and used in more than twenty countries. Consumers can scan bar codes on items and instantly find the best prices both online and based on their location. Marketers can include messages to a customer when an item is scanned, based on the customer's location and on the particular item scanned. A scanned CD, for example, could trigger a clip of the song with a message promoting the store where the customer is located. The message also might include a suggestion to join the company's loyalty program, offer a coupon on the spot, or buy tickets. The marketer pays based on how many people see the marketing message and how many people actually click or tap on it.

Jagtag. This company has created a leading 2D bar code that works with all camera phones. If the customer takes a picture of the code, an MMS message is sent to Jagtag; there the message is read and an MMS link is sent back to the phone. It was used for the *Sports Illustrated* Swimsuit Edition, so that the half dozen codes in the magazine could be scanned, resulting in a video being downloaded to the phone, which generated 120,000 customer engagements. "You can put different codes on products based on where they are sold," says Jagtag founder Dudley Fitzpatrick.[85]

SnapTag. From SpyderLink, in Colorado, come these customized codes that use a company's brand logo or product image by encircling it with code ring technology (basically, a circle with various small breaks that the company's technology recognizes and tracks). "This is a direct response opportunity [companies] didn't have before," says Jane McPherson, Chief Marketing Officer of SpyderLink.[86] The key is that the code can be read by any phone that has a camera and messaging capabilities; the image is sent as a message and recognized, so the appropriate message (text, video, etc.) is sent back. SpyderLink also provides the SnapTag Reader, making the reading–receiving process even faster and easier. Coors included SnapTags on its Coors packaging, letting age-appropriate customers snap and send the code, which automatically entered the sender in a contest to win various goodies, including tickets to the Super Bowl.

AT&T Code Scanner. This app can be used to scan most 2D bar code formats by aiming the phone's camera at the code. The app saves the last 100 scans, and you can access them again without re-scanning in the "History" location of the app. If you fill in the brief profile, you will receive notification of deals based on your location when you scan a code. The app is powered by the mobiletag decoder, from a leading European 2D bar code–reading company.

Microsoft Tag. This system provides information about how frequently and where tags were scanned by consumers. The information associated with tags, such as a link to a website, can be updated or changed at any time, even after the code is created and distributed; that is, tag information can be revised even after it has been printed on packaging. Microsoft Tags can commonly be read by other 2D bar code readers.

While it may be intriguing, or at least a bit of fun, to have a QR Code on a shirt, for brands and businesses there are other more substantive reasons to use 2D codes. As a marketer, you will need to decide how you want to use these codes and which ones are best for your purposes, as the market for scanning becomes more widespread. Following are several reasons the scanning market is poised to expand:

- The customer doesn't have to type anything to receive desired information.

- Code recognition technology will continue to improve.
- Multimedia messages can be sent instantly.
- Useful customer information can be provided.
- Information can be provided on location at exactly the right time, when the customer wants it.
- It is easy for a marketer to associate dramatically more information with products and packaging.
- Customers can receive value, making it worthwhile to scan codes.

One of the biggest drivers will be *the mobile chicken and egg phenomenon*. As more codes become visible on products, more consumers will wonder what they are. As more consumers point their cameras at the codes, more people will become curious about what they're doing. To get more customers to point their phones at these codes, marketers will provide added value to make it worth their while. One customer will tell another he can find a better price by scanning these codes. And as more customers start to use the codes, more marketers will be pushed to add them to *their* product packaging, to remain in line with the competition. This pattern will continue until the behavioral change is fully realized.

The 2D Bar Code Platform

One of the oldest of the 2D bar code companies is Scanbuy. The New York company was founded in 2001 and worked with the cell phone carriers and manufacturers at that time. Like other 2D bar code readers, Scanbuy's reader, called Scanlife, can read codes other than its own. Scanlife has been used all over the world and the company has active operations in the United States, Mexico, Chile, Spain, Italy, and Denmark, and the company's investors include Motorola Ventures.

These 2D codes will play an increasing role in the marketing and sales of products because they often are employed at the closest location to an actual purchase. "It was always about bar codes for us, but in 2007 mobile started to change and we moved to m-commerce," says David Javitch, Vice President of Marketing at Scanbuy.[87] "We were launching Beta programs with carriers at the time in preparation for mass adoption. We have different audiences, from consumers who use the app to scan all kinds of bar codes to businesses that can launch a campaign and track analytics from 120 million potential people in the U.S. alone."

While Scanbuy's bar code includes some of the common mobile bar code features, such as price comparison, it is the smallest-sized 2D bar code. Scanbuy is another example of a mobile company that has its underpinnings based on how its technology is used and the value of the information it provides back to the marketer. "It's a platform and a self-managed system, which virtually anyone can use from a large corporation down to a local business," says Javitch.

The Scanbuy system provides businesses with all the data from the scans, so they can see the number of scans, date, time of day, location, and demographics of the person scanning, such as age, gender, and income. "We get a 20 percent response rate on it," he says. "We're not relying on people to download an app. Verizon Wireless is placing codes all over their marketing material and they've had over 150,000 scans."

The value of using a 2D platform is the amount of information that can be captured as well as the amount that can be disseminated, since the code can be linked to any type of marketing material. Says Javitch:

> If it was Pepsi, for example, it (such as a website link) would go exactly where they want to go. Others are not taking a brand-down approach; for some it's only a price comparison approach. We will show that also to add value, but we let the brand control the content.
>
> Some customers think that linking to a basic website is enough, but that's not going to change a purchasing decision. But you start with baby steps like any new technology.
>
> There are brands that are serious about this. Verizon put an advertorial in *Travel & Leisure Magazine*. There were different ads about travel and movies.
>
> In the Verizon advertising they had hundreds of different codes. The value to Verizon is branding, since they want to show they're

betting on Android. It's a way to link people to the apps and a direct, visual link.

This is about discovery of content from a mobile device. Marketing is a huge piece of it. We're in the early days. We'll be able to send data in real time based on time and location. Tons of small and medium businesses are signing up. For example, realtors want to link to information on the properties.

The value is that this is the easiest way to get info from the physical world. They want to see more codes in the market. More 2D bar code software in the handsets will drive adoption, creating compelling use cases.

The next thing in 2D bar codes is commerce and instant gratification. You'll scan a code from a magazine, click to buy, and have it shipped. We're seeing a lot of purchases through Amazon with location-specific content. Restaurants are customizing content based on location, so they can allow two hours for a discount, for example.

We have more than ten million downloads of the app globally and expect ten million just in North America, and twenty-five million overall by the end of 2011.

A Scanbuy 2D code could link to a number of marketing messages, ranging from an instant coupon to a branded app. "Couponing type of applications are complicated because of the POS systems," says Javitch. "And getting installed base is very hard. But 2D looks better on an ad or anything on packaging and you need a sophisticated camera to read a UPC bar code."

As is typical with platforms in the mobile industry, Scanbuy captures the data and the brand accesses its data through the platform. And because of the speed of mobile and its always-on nature, brand managers can monitor their customer data as it happens.

Companies of all sizes are using 2D codes in a number of ways. Following are some examples of how some of Scanbuy's clients have been deploying 2D bar codes.

Heineken. Heineken printed EZcodes on its six-packs of beer, as part of its Know the Signs campaign. Once the code was scanned and the age of the buyer verified, an app called Breathalyzer could be instantly downloaded. The app works like this: a person notices a friend overconsuming alcohol; the phone's owner preselects from a list of characters (The Sleeper, the Groper, the Flirt, etc.) her friend most resembles when tipsy, then hands the phone to the friend; the friend blows into the phone microphone, the "breathalyzer," which shows that the person has had too much to drink (it does not truly function, of course); a humorous video showing the selected character in action launches. The EZ-code also links to another app called Taxi Magic that uses the smartphone location to show a list of taxi companies nearby. Select the taxi company, and the call is automatically placed.

Sears. The company placed 2D codes on more than four hundred different shelves for individual products. Each code linked a shopper to product specifications, consumer reviews, and an option to purchase. Thousands of shoppers scanned the codes, giving the sales staff another opportunity to interact with the customers.

Transantiago. This public transport system in Santiago, Chile, placed thousands of codes printed on stickers around the city at each bus stop, where commuters could sometimes endure lengthy waits for a specific bus. The codes linked to information about the current location of specific buses by using GPS locators already on the buses. The commuters could see when the bus was expected to arrive.

CB Richard Ellis. This commercial real estate property company, used codes on signage for its properties. The codes linked directly to a mobile page for that property with current pricing and agent contact information.

American Airlines. The airline placed 2D codes on outdoor media like billboards in major airports in the United States to drive users to its mobile site, which provided real-time flight status, gate information, and a reservation portal.

Morgan's Hotel Group. The hotel promoted its Twenty-Fifth Anniversary with a code that linked to a special discount of 10 percent off select stays and information on its hotel properties.

Nike. Nike placed 2D bar codes on special collector posters and in retail locations in Manila, in the Philippines, to promote its affiliation with the National Basketball Association and its new Developmental League. The design was intended to target teens and young adults through channels more integral to their way of life. In two months, Nike received thirty thousand scans, forty-two thousand content downloads, and ninety-six thousand page views of its mobile site, all from the 2D bar codes.

Volkswagen. The car maker placed 2D codes on its national brochures for the GTI and Golf. Each code linked to a different experience, including a driving video, additional photos, and a connection to VW's soccer affiliation.

The Reality of Augmented Reality

Combining mobile technology and the physical world opens many possibilities for more seamlessly merging the two, or at least for allowing them to better supplement each other. This is the idea behind what is known as *augmented reality*, which, as its name implies, involves augmenting, or adding more information, to the reality in front of you.

If a person points the camera of a smartphone toward the Golden Gate Bridge, for example, an augmented reality view would show her the history of the bridge, statistics on the number of cars that pass over it annually, and so on, as an overlay for the image on the phone. This merging of the reality that's in front of a person with digital data or images provides what I call *onsite insight*. This data overlay can lead to a new object awareness, wherein a previously static or even boring-looking object can be brought to life by the new context given to it via mobile.

Mobile companies are already innovating in this area, adding information and images to static objects. An Amsterdam-based company called Layar launched an augmented reality app for GPS-enabled smartphones that overlays images or interactive three-dimensional objects. For instance, a person selects the "layar" (what the company calls its overlays) of Twitter users nearby and the one for restaurants nearby; when the person points his phone's camera lens at a set of buildings, images or dots appear over the landscape, showing locations of nearby people tweeting and nearby restaurants. Launching the compass layar adds an overlay on the phone screen showing the direction of the object being viewed in relation to the viewer. The app has been downloaded by millions of people. And, not to be outdone, Google introduced an augmented reality service called Google Goggles, which allows a smartphone owner to take a photo of something, such as a book or painting, and automatically be provided with a web link with information on that object.

From a marketer's point of view, augmented reality can offer one more way to reach untethered consumers. For example, a quick-service restaurant could augment reality with a virtual map of its locations that includes a 3D photo of an appealing meal, appropriate to the time of day.

Augmented reality can be highly useful when there is a lot of data pertaining to a given product or service. This is the case with certain buildings and landmarks, as historical data can easily be associated with such places. Sporting events are another example where statistics abound but are not readily available to those at the game, though people listening to radio or watching on TV get lots of facts from announcers, who are fed stats to pass along to viewers.

One organization currently contemplating potential uses for augmented reality is the PGA Tour. "Augmented reality may be used in the near term by the PGA," says David Plant, Director of Mobile, PGA Tour.[88] "Every shot that a player hits is tracked by laser. What if we could take that data so that fans on site could see the information on the golfer? Like what percentage are they from this location? And we could include the location of facilities on site for fans. With location-based, what if we can identify by merchandise and drive additional sales?"

It is this type of a well-defined set of benefits that will drive mobile technologies such as augmented reality. It's not the technology, but rather the benefits it can bring that will lead to a change in consumer behavior.

As in other areas of a world gone mobile, it will not necessarily be the technology that holds businesses and marketers back from using mobile innovations to better serve their customers. It's more likely that mobile will be circumscribed by traditional ways of thinking, ingrained habits, or lack of integration of technology with legacy systems. In the case of the PGA, for example, a major hurdle to overcome has nothing to do with the availability of golfer statistics, budget, or augmented reality programs. People are not allowed to carry cell phones on PGA courses.

More Efficiency with Finding

In a world gone mobile, the finders will provide great value to untethered consumers. Finders will make life easier, since it will be faster and more efficient for customers to retrieve the precise information they are looking for at the moment based on where they are. They will be able to compare products and prices and find the best value based on where they are and what they're doing. Savvy companies will take advantage of these new mobile capabilities, as long as they add value to the customer experience.

And while they are on location, many consumers will check in to let their friends know where they are, as mobile goes social.

Social Goes Mobile

CHAPTER 8

Watch moviegoers at the end of a movie reach for their phones as they amble out of the theater. They're plugging back into their mobile, social networks to see what they may have missed during the movie. Untethered consumers not only feel comfortable with all-the-time social networking, but also recognize that they are part of the network, no matter where they are or what they're doing.

Untethered consumers have the ability to let friends and others know where they are, what they are doing, and when they are doing it. They also want to be aware of where *their* friends are, what *they* are doing, and when *they* are doing it. Mobile makes all this possible.

Internet use is not just about access to the almost infinite amount of information and knowledge available, it's about communication with new and old friends through digital interactions. It's about connecting to and being connected to others. And for marketers, there is opportunity (and challenges) in knowing when and how to participate or add value to their customers within these connections.

And since friends decide how to communicate with friends, they ultimately select which mobile social media platform works best for them. Marketers then have to decide where their customers and potential customers digitally reside and determine how to reach them in those venues. One of the key reasons marketers need to participate in these mobile connections is because it is where their current and potentially future customers digitally congregate.

Mobile as Social Platform

There's no doubt that mobile will become a dominant vehicle for social networking. More than 200 million people already access Facebook through their mobile phones.[89] Also, people who use Facebook on their mobile devices are twice as active on Facebook as nonmobile users, and there are more than two hundred mobile operators in sixty countries working to deploy and promote Facebook mobile products.

About a fifth of mobile phone owners in the United States have used a social networking site on their phone in 2010, double the number from the previous year.[90] And those with smartphones are significantly heavier users of social media on mobile, with more than half of smartphone owners using mobile social media compared to fewer than one in ten of those with regular phones.

As is the case with social media in general, Facebook is the largest draw on mobile, attracting 89 percent of those using social media via mobile, with 39 percent using MySpace via mobile, 29 percent using Twitter, and 12 percent using LinkedIn.[91] Untethered consumers use their phones to post comments, visit friends' profiles, update their statuses, browse profiles, receive updates by text messages, post photos, search for friends, and add events.

Traditional social networking platforms are moving to mobile, which will be larger than PC-based social networking, because of its ease of use and always-on nature. Mobile applications have been created for the social media platforms such as Facebook and Twitter, facilitating more social networking on the fly and in real time. Social media is generating a great deal of buzz in business today, and the convergence of social networking and mobile devices is a natural progression that will likely lead to a sort of "social networking on steroids."

In one year, total minutes spent on social networking sites in the United States increased 83 percent and total minutes spent on Facebook increased nearly 700 percent. Consumers hear of trends via their social networks, and businesses already challenged to reach consumers via traditional social media will be even more challenged to insert their products and services into the mobile social scene.

Location Awareness

In addition to traditional social media platforms such as Facebook and Twitter, there also are location-based services (LBS) devoted to social media, and these allow friends and associates to be tracked and to track each other, essentially letting one another know where they are at a given moment.

Some users may feel somewhat self-conscious to realize that others know where they are or that their movements are being tracked. However, the consumer generally has to "check in" at a location to register his whereabouts; that is, the user must click or tap on his phone to announce that he is at a place. The phone, of course, "knows" where the consumer is and typically provides several options for check-in. For example, if a person is at a bank next to a Pizza Hut that is next to a salon, all locations might be offered and the consumer selects the one where he is actually located.

The general idea is that friends can see where their friends are. These services' initial popularity was in large cities like New York, San Francisco, and Chicago, and it grew from there. This is where the potential marketing opportunity comes in. By offering value to current and especially future customers, businesses with physical locations can offer incentives. They can reward customers for introducing their friends to the particular location, increasing word-of-mouth marketing of friends to each other. Marketers can also encourage people to try a product or service by offering first-time-visit deals, for example, both to new customers and friends of regular customers, via those friends. Marketers will be faced with deciding which of the location-based social mobile services to engage and which of the location-based marketing strategies is the best match for the company's goals. Participating in these social mobile networks is different than location-based marketing. With location-based marketing, the communication is between the company and the customer. With social mobile, the conversation is between mobile friends based on location, and marketers engage within that conversation. The biggest opportunity for a marketer may be to create a brand new customer program; location-based platforms have only been around for a few years, and there are undoubtedly many possibilities for reaching and enticing consumers that haven't even been conceived yet. Even given their relatively recent arrival, location-based programs have already attracted millions of untethered consumers, who are participating and being rewarded to varying degrees.

These services also provide consumers with psychological rewards, such as badges for checking in a number of times at a particular location or other elite status for going to certain places or doing certain things. The services can also encourage friendly competition among friends and even strangers, to achieve a certain status. One slight issue with the location-based services is that they typically notify friends when you check in but not when you leave, so a friend may think you are in a location but you already left.

The services can also be useful at very large events: even when a user does not know many people there, he can see where groups are congregating at any given moment, because he can view activity by location. No personal information is typically shared with those not designated as friends.

Self-Aggregation

Located in a six-story building in Cooper Square in lower Manhattan, Foursquare has become one of the more popular location-based services. Early in 2010, the company subleased space from another start-up company on the fifth floor of the building. On that floor, employees of three separate companies worked side by side in front of large computer screens. Against the backdrop of a few bicycles parked inside the office, a dozen or so programmers—many wearing headphones—quietly focused on their specific tasks.

As Foursquare grew, it leased additional space from the *Village Voice*, headquartered on the third floor, and workers alternated working on different floors, depending on the week. After the company raised $20 million from venture capitalists, it renovated the entire sixth floor of the building, with panoramic views of the city. The three companies then moved to the top floor, though Foursquare went from lessee to lessor.

Foursquare is not about its own real estate, but rather about the physical spaces inhabited by its users at any given moment. It is a social networking platform from which people can check in and broadcast their locations as they move through the world. Mobile users' phones know approximately where they are, and can offer choices of locations in the immediate area; to check in, the untethered consumer simply selects the one where she is currently located. If her location is not listed, she can search and either find it quickly or enter it (for example, if the location is a new store or restaurant), which helps Foursquare grow organically.

Millions of people use Foursquare, and they get credit in one form or another for "checking in." Within its first sixteen months, there were a hundred million checked-ins on Foursquare. Only two months later, that number hit two hundred million check-ins. That's more than a million and a half check-ins a day at one place or another.

Consumers also have the option to link their Foursquare account with other social networking services they may use. For example, if a person links his Foursquare account to Twitter, each time that person checks in, the system can send an automatic tweet to his followers, letting them know where he is.

Some of the rewards are designed to create fun, local competition. For example, if a person checks in more than anyone else at a location within a certain period of time, she becomes the "Mayor" of that location. Besides earning bragging rights, the "Mayor" may be eligible for rewards from marketers. After all, what business would not want to offer a little something extra to its most frequent visitors?

So there are two distinct sides to social media on mobile, a consumer side and a business side. "On the consumer side, you have a group of people who are connected by what I call ambient awareness," says Eric Friedman, Director of Client Services at Foursquare.[92] "It's really an added layer of awareness. It might be a ten-person circle; that is the value proposition. And it involves younger people and adults alike. For the consumers, it's about discovery. For example, you can check what's going on in different cities. You become mayor by visiting more times than anyone else within sixty days. Foursquare is basically an interactive city guide. The idea is you only get things that interest you. With Foursquare, you can highlight local restaurants in New York. It could be a trip or a place to visit, with a tip tied to a way to check in."

The movements of those using Foursquare are visible only to the people that the users allow as their "friends," which they can delete at any time. As a result, there could be thousands of different groups of friends, but each person follows and is followed by only his own connections. A person can also go somewhere and not check in, since it is entirely optional. "Privacy requires a symmetrical relationship," says Friedman, "You have to ask and accept friendship. The key for consumers is ambient awareness or passive awareness of where their friends are."

Platforms such as Foursquare facilitate mobile social community. While mobile consumers could send a text message to their friends, telling them where they are in case friends are also in the neighborhood, it would be tedious to do so on a recurring basis. Foursquare makes it easy and instant. The service also keeps track of check-in locations for a person, which the user can view at any time, and it awards badges, such as "Local," "Super User," and "Gym Rat," for checking in at various types of locations a certain number of times.

As phones get "smarter," it gets easier to check in. While services such as Foursquare have been popular with early adopters for a while, they have now attracted millions of users who are checking in regularly during the course of their days and nights. These social networking services ultimately provide merchants with an opportunity to reward their best customers, as well as appeal to new ones. "There are two constituencies that most businesses want to target: new customers and loyal customers," says Friedman. "We're at the very nascent stages of location-based services."

Foursquare can be considered more of a platform than an agency, because it allows other mobile companies to add applications and to integrate their services with Foursquare.

Hyperlocal Marketing

The opportunity for marketers and merchants is to reach customers closer to their brands, products, and services, and to engage with them in a more meaningful way. Businesses need to experiment—test and learn—to see what works best for their customers.

For example, in its first test of Foursquare, Starbucks offered a one dollar discount on a Frappuccino to any Mayor of Starbucks. However, at checkout, some Starbucks employees had no knowledge of Foursquare nor what a Mayor was. This is an issue that large companies face, whether they are using Foursquare or another location-based service. Over time, based on incentives offered, businesses have seen their customer use of location-based services grow, and as use reaches a critical mass, companies will be charged with making sure their employees understand the full range of marketing messages and incentives the brand is using.

Starbucks also faced the issue of some employees becoming the Mayor of the stores in which they worked, as they could check in at any time; because the employees are there many days a week, it was easy for them to usurp the place of frequent customers. Some considered that practice to be cheating.

Another issue Starbucks faced was lack of targeting. If the Mayor was a loyal hot cappuccino drinker, the Frappuccino offer may have been wasted. However, that is the point of a test-and-learn approach: to see what works and what doesn't, get customer feedback, and modify the program to best serve customers. Without this test-and-learn knowledge, Starbucks would still be at square one. Following are some possibilities that Starbucks or similar merchants who are using mobile social networks might feature:

- Ask the Mayors to vote daily or weekly on what they prefer to drink.
- Show the Mayors (and others when they check in to Starbucks on Foursquare) what menu items Mayors nationwide prefer.
- Have the Mayors vote, by region, on what drinks should be discounted for the Mayors that week.
- Reward loyalty: Tier frequent visitors and offer deals for more frequent check-ins, even if the user has not reached Mayor status.

- Highlight each Starbucks Mayor's preferred drink of the week at each location.
- Highlight the preferred drinks of all the Foursquare Starbucks check-ins each week.
- Reward a first-time check-in with a discount coupon for the next visit.

With Foursquare, merchants usually walk before they run. "It typically starts with small involvement and then it grows," says Foursquare's Eric Friedman. "We work on building out relationship management. Merchants can create loyalty offers, such as 'Check in once and get a free entrée.' In the case of Whole Foods, they have stores where they have window stickers promoting Foursquare. They accumulate data anonymously."

Foursquare has established partnerships with more than ten thousand businesses of all types and sizes. "We have a mix of small merchants and large companies such as *The Wall Street Journal*. We have a woman with a chocolate shop on the West Coast." Friedman projects exponential growth as more people acquire smartphones and more businesses offer incentives to their customers via the Foursquare self-serve dashboard.

"Foursquare is a platform," says Friedman. "There will be ubiquity of smart devices. This is analogous to search and search marketing. With Google and AdWords, they got millions of advertisers," he says, referring to the Google program that lets businesses create and post their own advertising messages. "If you look at the ad funnel, you had traditional ads; coming down, you then had view and click, further down, search. With print you had no accountability. With TV there was some. Search shows intent. But location-based has real accountability. It's discovery, like a city guide that's interactive."

As the technological platform and behavioral aspects evolve over time, more useful information will become available to both consumers and businesses. "For travel, there can be predictive modeling and suggestions," says Friedman. "And for businesses there is data exhaust, which can be used in aggregate to see categorically where people come from and perhaps where they might be going next."

The advantage for consumers is that they can see where their friends are and where they go. For marketers, the opportunity will be to reach out and interact with those groups of mobile friends and to provide substantial value to them.

Marketing with Location-Based Services

While Foursquare creates and provides the LBS platform, it's up to marketers to decide how to use such platforms. The good news is that many of these and other platforms in the mobile industry are designed for self-service. The marketer can often sign up and start marketing almost immediately using simple online tools provided by the mobile companies. While some businesses choose simple promotions, such as a one-time discount to a first-time visitor or recurring discounts for the Mayor, others go deep, integrating their current business and loyalty systems with various social networking platforms.

Tasti D-Lite was founded in New York in 1987 as a purveyor of lower-calorie frozen desserts, and grew quickly to more than sixty independently owned and operated stores in and around the New York City area. In 2007, the company was acquired by a New York private equity firm that brought in as CEO Jim Amos, who grew Mail Boxes Etc. to five thousand locations before it was sold to UPS.

By the end of 2010, the company was moving internationally into South Korea, Mexico, and the United Arab Emirates and was expanding aggressively in the United States, with plans to open more than three hundred locations around the country. But before Tasti D-Lite's dramatic expansion, it established the foundation for loyalty growth among all the company's customers, and a critical component of that program involves social networking via mobile.

Early in 2010, Tasti D-Lite launched its TastiRewards loyalty program, which rewards members for their purchases. Customers register their TreatCard online and earn points for purchases made at Tasti D-Lite locations. The program is believed to be the first social media–enabled rewards program that allowed members to opt in and have their accounts automatically send messages by Foursquare or Twitter when they earned or redeemed points. BJ Emerson, Social Technology

Officer at Tasti D-Lite, says, "We got involved with Foursquare early on because we saw that our customers were checking in on Foursquare at Tasti D-Lite venues.[93] We thought, 'Here's an opportunity for us to engage with our customers and reward them for their digital activity.'"

When businesses examine the mobile use patterns of their customers, it often becomes painfully obvious what they should do. But it's obvious only if they look. In many cases, a company's customers are participating in the mobile revolution and the company remains unaware. "If you see activity that your customers are talking about you or checking in with your brand, product, or service, why aren't you engaging with them?" says Emerson. "Are you even listening?" According to Emerson:

> In one instance, we had a location opening in Arizona and the franchisee got on Facebook and had six hundred group members before he even opened his doors. There is great opportunity if you're listening and are willing to engage. With the real-time nature of these communities, it's not unheard of to even catch consumers in the middle of a purchase decision.
>
> Many online networks such as Yelp and Facebook now have mobile features. Before, you had visibility to the conversations but now the activity is getting more local and granular. Customers are checking in to venues and most business owners have no clue that this virtual activity is taking place.
>
> You can walk into any strip mall in America and access Foursquare or any number of other location-based services on a smartphone and see all the reviews and tips people have left at the different establishments.
>
> There are also gaming elements within these applications. Friends can earn badges and compete against each other to become Mayor, then oust each other when they check in more often.
>
> For us, it's all about new customer acquisition and rewarding existing customers. We saw that our customers were already talking about Tasti D-Lite online and we simply wanted to put a mechanism in place to reward them for their digital activity.

As to driving business and building brand awareness, we can easily show that the publishing of the automated TastiRewards messages are potentially going out to thousands of people's friends and followers. Customers are marketing to their friends and followers on behalf of Tasti D-Lite by sharing their loyalty activity and many are learning about Tasti D-Lite for the first time through these social channels.

A lot of businesses get the importance of this, but *how* to execute on this type of program is the key. There are obviously some technological barriers in setting up a program like this. All locations have to have the same POS (point of sale) system and the same loyalty program processor.

Our loyalty program works across all participating locations and the transaction data is fully integrated with our POS systems. We started three years prior, moving all of the locations to the same platform so we could support a national gift and loyalty card program.

The integration of Tasti D-Lite's POS system with its loyalty card and Foursquare programs makes the customer experience and interaction relatively seamless. If a person uses his loyalty card, it can automatically check him in on Foursquare. If he checks in at a Tasti D-Lite location on Foursquare, it can credit his loyalty card.

It is critical for businesses to link established systems, such as point of sale and loyalty programs, to apps used by mobile customers. Marketers and business leaders first need to think through all the elements of the customer experience, including the kinds of messages that should be sent.

Tasti D-Lite has two types of automated loyalty messages: messages that say something like "Sorry about this automated message, but I just earned ten points at Tasti D-Lite and I had to tell someone," and those that let friends know when a user receives a free reward. Customers have an incentive to participate because they receive extra points when they enable the messages. Separately, the customer receives a point for each dollar he spends. When he earns fifty points, he can get a free cup or cone. He also receives an extra point when they post on each network he is connected to.

Here's an exchange about Tasti-D-Lite that occurred on Twitter:

SARAH: "I'm at Tasti D-Lite in Nashville and I bet I got more Tasti-Rewards points than you." [Includes link to one-dollar discount coupon.]

BETSIE: "Why does it tweet every time you go to Tasti-D-Lite?"

SARAH: "Because it gives me extra points to get to my free tasti cup: duh!"

The next step for Tasti D-Lite is to build customer incentives. Emerson envisions generating unique coupons for a customer's friends, which would add value to the customer's Twitter stream. "We would make it so the coupon is specific to the person who sent it. When redeemed, the sender can get a referral point," he says. "We're then incenting everybody." There are technical challenges to overcome, however. Says Emerson:

From a format standpoint, the [loyalty] card simply identifies the account so that the transaction is associated with the customer. We could change the format to a bar code displayed on a smartphone, so that you pull up an image and put it under a scanner, which would then identify them. Customers are not quite there yet, but it's just a matter of time. It will also take an investment in new POS scanner hardware.

For many years we used a punch card for rewards, and then moved to a plastic card. It would be quite a leap for some of our customers to move exclusively to swiping smartphones at this point, but we have seen that it can be different in some new markets that we go into.

You have to see if the demographic fits the digital profile. The response in certain cities in Florida is different than, say, in Houston. In Florida, with older customers, we're having to do some things differently, like register them at the POS terminal as opposed to having them register online.

For Tasti D-Lite, mobile is all about customer activity, customer incentive, and customer data. The company captures data on customers' favorite flavors and registers inactivity as well. "If they're not here for sixty days, we have the opportunity to send an SMS message to them," says Emerson.

There are a number of location-based services that allow various elements of check-in, commentary on places and things, and connecting capabilities. Following is a sampling:

Facebook Places. Not to be outdone by the primarily location-based services, Facebook launched its own location-based application, called Places, which allows its hundreds of millions of users to check in and let their friends know where they are. Facebook also permitted the integration of some other social media platforms, such as Foursquare and Gowalla, so that check-ins could work across platforms. Initially there were no incentives, such as badges or titles, associated with checking in through the Facebook app. However, Facebook ultimately introduced a program for retailers and merchants to offer deals through the mobile application. In one, for example, the Gap offered a free pair of jeans to the first 10,000 people who checked in to their local Gap store using Facebook's mobile app.

Loopt. Loopt continually updates a person's location when she checks in at a location with her phone. Information about a person's location is automatically shared with friends, based on the length of time the person chooses to be visible after checking in. Friends allow friends to see where they are located. Loopt Mix allows mobile consumers to browse profiles of interesting people near them and post status updates to introduce themselves. Based in Palo Alto, California, Loopt boasts more than four million registered users. Marketers can create customized rewards to drive more traffic to a business, as well as use targeted advertising tied to certain locations.

Brightkite. This service provides levels of badges based on various activities, such as a mobile check-in at a location or posting a number of photos. Founded in 2005, this Burlingame, California, company allows customers to enter sweepstakes based on checking in at specific stores. Consumers using the service can leave tips, such as what foods they liked and reviews of locations they visited, and can include photos. Brightkite provides marketers the ability to track high relevance, such as people within a certain number of miles, and to reach them with a specific offer at a certain time.

Gowalla. This mobile app allows people to share their favorite places with friends around the world. People can share and view photos and can accept and reject friends on the fly. Based in Austin, Texas, Gowalla was launched in 2009, and uses the phone's location to share a person's whereabouts with friends and to generate targeted marketing text messages that the person might find appealing. Marketers can create special "Gowalla trips" that highlight attractions for a person to visit, which can drive more customers to a specific business.

Gilroy. Gilroy enables conversations in real time based on the location of the person. Rather than showing what all friends are saying on social networks, Gilroy shows content based on proximity. So at a sporting event, for example a baseball game, a person would see and interact only with those attending the game. It also allows a person to search by location to see what people near that location are discussing online at the moment.

SCVNGR. This is a location-based social game about going places, competing in challenges, and earning points. A challenge at a location may be taking a photo or leaving a comment, and players earn badges for challenges completed. People can also create their own challenges based on a location. Marketers can give rewards based on activity accomplished at a location and may include deadlines for redemption.

Whrll. Whrll is designed for groups of people with shared passions. It allows a user to check in to discover "Societies" and find others with similar interests. Users can choose who their check-ins are shared with (friends only, the public), upload photos, and earn points for special offers, called "Society Rewards," from businesses.

Marketers can use these rewards as a loyalty program and can offer special deals based on the number of check-ins within a certain period of time.

The Race to Installed Base

When the fax machine was first used, it was not widely accepted, in part because not everyone had one. If you had a fax machine and no one you knew had it, yours had virtually no value. As fax machines proliferated in businesses, however, their value increased.

Once fax machines became ubiquitous, their value was dramatically higher than when there were few machines. This is the law of the installed base: Once adoption reaches critical mass, the product or services attain maximum value. At some point, any business without a fax machine was forced to get one, so it could operate within the installed base.

Social media platforms on mobile are in a race to create a large installed base, because those with the largest number of people using them will become the likely vehicles for marketing messages, which will help fund the underlying platforms and their growth.

Businesses themselves also are embracing the idea of allowing their customers to check in using their own brands as incentives. So rather than customers using one of the public platforms, such as Foursquare or Gowalla, a brand may incent customers to use the brands' own preferred platform, either their own or another they select. For example, InterContinental Hotels Group joined the Topguest program, which aggregates various social mobile platforms, so that it could provide its Priority Club members additional loyalty points when they check in through the major social media platforms, based on location at one of the chain's more than four thousand hotels.

Using social media platforms from mobile phones can take advantage of USPT by leveraging the real-time and location advantages of mobile. The key, for you as a marketer, is to determine which platforms your customers are using and to follow them to those platforms. Creative programs that excite and engage customers on mobile platforms come from marketers, not from the platforms themselves.

The platform technology enables the programs to operate, but it can't create meaningful content and customer interaction.

There are additional ways to interact with those customers by launching a text or video campaign to allow your customers to opt in to the push–pull of mobile, which we discuss in the next chapter.

CHAPTER 9

The Push–Pull of Mobile

Mobile is both a push and a pull medium. As a marketer, you can push information, such as advertising messages and offers. It's not quite broadcast, because the messages are more tailored to specific categories of untethered consumers rather than pushed out using the mass-market approach of television commercial broadcasts.

On the other side, m-powered consumers can pull information, such as product ratings or information updates, from almost anywhere at will. They can pull information from one another, from product reviews, and from your company, assuming you have promotional material that provides the customer with value.

One of the most effective ways for marketers to interact with mobile customers is by exchanging messages with those willing to communicate with your company.

The Pull of SMS Marketing

While the exponential growth of smartphones continues, there are times when it's appropriate to deploy traditional SMS (Short Message Service), or text, messaging, even if the majority of your customers are using the most sophisticated of handheld devices. This is a great example of the UPT approach, which allows you to reach significantly more people because almost anyone can receive text messages, while not everyone can download a sophisticated location-based app.

Despite all the creativity and activity surrounding smartphone technology, SMS also continues to grow. For example, in 2005 there were 81 billion SMS messages transmitted in the United States.[94] By 2009, the number of SMS messages sent grew to 1.6 trillion. The total number of SMS messages expected to be sent globally this year is seven trillion.[95]

Marketers know that to send SMS messages, they must get the potential customer to opt in, or agree to receive specific types of messages from them.[96] This process prevents consumers from receiving unwanted messages or spam on their cell phones. Untethered consumers view their mobile phones as personal, and they do not want uninvited people or businesses intruding in that space.

To opt in, customers text a word selected by the marketer to a code that is generally five or six numbers in length. For example, a marketer might ask a customer to text "Contest" to 642432. A marketer typically would include this code in traditional advertising, place it on the company's website, and, depending on the company, include it on product packaging. This type of opt-in program is much easier for large brands with wide distribution, because the invitation to opt in can be easily spread (on, for example, bottle caps or soft drink cans). A smaller business also can spread the word with in-store signage, e-mail messages, or notes printed on receipts.

A customer who opts in receives a response from the marketer that makes the offer clear; the opt-in is also often followed by a request for e-mail confirmation that the customer does indeed want to receive this type of marketing message. For many individuals, text messages are viewed as one-to-one messages between themselves and someone they know, and they may be resistant to allowing companies to encroach on this territory. Because of the challenge a marketer may face in penetrating this circle, the value or potential value offered to the customer has to be very high. The upside is that the people who do opt in tend to have high interest or to really want whatever is being offered, even if it's just the potential to win a desired prize.

GLOSSARY

MMS. Multimedia Messaging Service. Can include pictures, sounds, and video with text, and the messages are receivable on a wide range of phones.

opt-in. A customer's agreement to participate. For a marketer to engage in a two-way interaction for a mobile promotion, the customer has to consent, usually by texting a message using the short code provided by the marketer. Double opt-in is best, in which the person opts in and the company asks for an additional confirmation.

opt-out. A customer's right to stop participating. If a marketer sends excessive or useless text promos, this is what customers will do. The mobile subscriber texts "stop" or "remove" to the short code, and then is removed from the database. The marketer needs to make it very easy for people to opt out.

SMS. Short Message Service. Mobile text messages that can be up to 160 characters long. Marketers can use SMS to send targeted text messages to subscribers' mobile phones, once they opt in.

SMS text. The short text messages customers can send to one another or to the company once they opt in to the promotion.

When customers opt in, it means they have found you and asked (or at least agreed) to hear about a specific topic, product, service, opportunity, or event. They agree to interact with you, up close and personal. There are mobile companies in various locations that you can use to deploy SMS marketing, for example, Open Market in Washington, iLoop Mobile in California, GoLive Mobile in Colorado, and Express Text in Illinois, to name a few.

One of the pioneering SMS messaging companies is mobileStorm, based in Los Angeles, California. The company was founded in 1999 by Jared Reitzin, the company's CEO and Chairman. "When we first started, we couldn't get people too excited, there was no consumer adoption," says Reitzin.[97] "Two or three years ago it started taking off, because everyone purchased a cell phone. Also the cost to text came down a lot and flat rate plans were introduced."

The large SMS growth for mobileStorm started around the time of the iPhone launch and that platform's subsequent growth. Reitzin sees a distinct difference between the two, with apps competing with SMS, to some degree. "With SMS you get someone to opt in to the database, but with a mobile app anybody can just download it and use it once," he says. "All marketers should have a multichannel strategy. They can use SMS to upgrade their app and you can install it from SMS so you can have a call to action."

Marketers should consider both SMS and apps, depending on their objectives and where their customers reside on mobile. In the course of our research for this book, we found highly successful examples of each approach. "Ultimately, it is best to use both," says Reitzin. Mobile apps are very saturated and costly to develop and maintain. The choice really depends on the marketer's needs, but both SMS and apps have their place.

Just as banner ads still reside on the Web after all these years, early marketing efforts on mobile, like SMS, will continue to exist. This is not to say that there are not better ways to market on the Web than banner ads, just as there are better ways than SMS to market on mobile, depending on the situation. If you're looking to reach a specific demographic that primarily uses iPhones, then an app and a mobile website may be the best approach. If you're looking to reach a demographic that's not yet smartphone saturated, then SMS marketing could make more sense.

With mobile, there often are multiple marketing choices, depending on the target market and the desired outcome. The choice comes down to using UPT or USPT, or both. Over time, customers' expectations will rise, as mobile technology and networks continue to improve and put more capabilities directly into the hands of the consumer. But both UPT and USPT approaches can dramatically increase company-to-customer interactivity.

One-Time Event Mobile Marketing

SMS can be especially effective for one-time promotions or events, when you want to entice your customers to *do* something. This is what I call *one-time event mobile marketing*. The objective is highly focused, with a beginning and an end, the end being the sale or service day. Unlike overall mobile marketing, this technique is designed for special events. Of course, you can repeat the process and conduct other special events on other days.

Whether you are conducting an ongoing mobile program or promoting a one-time event, you have to give the customer a compelling reason to interact with you. Technologies and platforms such as the SMS messaging services provided by mobileStorm simply enable and facilitate mobile marketing. It is still up to marketers to conceive the best methods and approaches for their customers and to design customer experiences that provide superior value.

The clients mobileStorm has attracted are wide ranging, and include *American Idol*, Kaiser Permanente, Qantas, NASCAR, New Balance, Chicken Soup for the Soul, Humana, Ashley Furniture Home-Stores, and Hooters Casino Hotel. Marketing objectives drive the SMS programs, usually with up-front objectives and expectations. Following are examples of the ways some of mobileStorm's customers have used SMS and their results.

Cars Sold. Fox Chevrolet in Timonium, Maryland, sold thirty-four cars in a single day through a mobile marketing program meant to drive consumers into the auto dealer's lot. Fox Chevrolet bought ten- and fifteen-second promotions on a Baltimore radio station, and encouraged people to text in for a chance to win a ninety-eight-dollar car. Nearly five hundred listeners texted the keyword FOX to the station's short code, with about three hundred attending a day-long promotional event that resulted in the sale of seventeen new cars and seventeen used cars, in addition to the two ninety-eight-dollar used cars that were awarded. Traditionally, automobiles have been sold through mass media, including television and print advertising, a dated approach in a world gone mobile. The dealer measured the effectiveness of the campaign via sales and foot traffic.

Building a Database. Cosmetics company Clinique used mobile to activate its print campaign within Bon-Ton stores, a chain of department stores based in York, Pennsylvania, that operates more than two hundred stores in more than twenty states throughout the country. As part of its Free Seven-Piece Gift Set giveaway, Clinique added a mobile call to action in a printed circular, asking consumers to text the keyword GIFT to short code 266866 to receive exclusive text alerts for upcoming gift offers. Clinique was able to build a sizeable mobile database for future marketing efforts.

Clothing Couponing. Planet Funk, a California-based chain of fashion clothing with more than twenty stores, faced a challenging holiday season. The company launched a mobile coupon offer for Black Friday by promoting short codes and keywords on signs in the stores and on their website, as well as on the websites of malls where its stores were located. By the end of the campaign, Planet Funk found that 20 percent of its sales had come from the mobile coupons. Close to two thousand coupons were generated, with a redemption rate of 91 percent. Of those who redeemed the coupons, 15 percent opted in to participate in future mobile campaigns.

Secret Sales. Ashley Furniture HomeStores of Charlotte, North Carolina, created a four-day secret sale announced only to message subscribers. It sent six thousand text messages announcing the sale on the first day of the sales event. The text messages generated $85,438 in revenue.

Restaurant Contest. Hooters of America ran a national mobile sweepstakes promoted in 380 of the restaurant chain's U.S. locations. The text-to-win promotion gave Hooters customers the chance to win a trip for two to Las Vegas to meet country music singer Kenny Chesney during a concert at the Hard Rock Hotel and Casino. Hooters partnered with Chesney's NoShoesRadio.com to host the promotion, which consumers could enter by texting the keyword KENNY to short code 36832. In less than a month, seventy-five hundred mobile consumers opted in to the Hooters Mobile Club. The company earlier used mobile in the launch of a national promotion aimed at building the Hooters Mobile Club, which grew to more than fifty thousand members. Signs in the restaurants invited customers to text the keyword POOL to short code 36832 to enter to win a trip to a Super Pool Party in Miami. The text-message marketing in its video-on-demand commercial spots resulted in a 32 percent increase in sales during the program.

As short codes evolve, in the future they may involve taking a picture rather than typing codes. Another evolution is from Zoove.com, a company that created a system that allows untethered consumers to type two asterisks followed by a word, such as **COKE, which then provides a link to whatever the marketer designated. The link could be to a mobile site, an app, a special offer, or a video, for example. No matter the technique used to make the connection, the customer still has to consciously agree. "If there's no opt-in process, you don't control the database," says mobileStorm's Jared Reitzin. "With SMS, there can be a call to action. But for opt-in, you need to be very cautious about frequency. A deal-of-the day is OK as long as it's clear and the customer is receptive."

No one yet knows how many programs and offers m-powered consumers will opt in to, or whether they will experience overload as the number of options increases. However, the critical factor will continue to be the level of value you provide to make it worth it for customers to keep interacting with your brand.

In many of those interactions, perhaps based on location or even on specific activity at the moment, there is another pull aspect of mobile. "There's a conversation you can have over SMS and social, a two-way dialogue," says Reitzin. "Companies can use SMS alongside social."

Like other companies that provide SMS, Reitzin's organization has to figure out how to accommodate the growing role of mobile video and how to integrate it into messaging campaigns. "Mobile video is going to get bigger and bigger. Slow network speeds and lack of 3G handsets have stifled growth, but it's coming. Thirty-five percent of phones are now smartphones and that number is going to double in just a short couple of years," he says.

Because of the nature of opt-in marketing, one of the assets that results from SMS is a highly relevant and targeted customer database. Over the past five years, Reitzin's company alone has sent billions of text and e-mail messages.

The Lure of MMS Marketing

In addition to reaching mobile customers via SMS, or text messages, marketers can send them content in a richer form through MMS, which stands for Multimedia Messaging Service. As the name implies, MMS facilitates the transmission of different forms of media, such as photos and video, directly to mobile phones.

Many consumers have naturally figured out that MMS is for things besides text, since when they take a picture with their phone, that's what they use to send it to others. What many customers may not know is that, unlike the 160-character limit of text messaging with SMS, there is no such limit for MMS messages.

Marketers using only SMS at times bump into the 160-character limitation, though SMS experts generally help figure ways around that. For example, when marketing a special deal to customers using SMS, it's not professional or appealing to abbreviate "If u come 2 our restaurant w/in next hr ...," rather than sending a well-crafted (or at least completely worded) offer. Of course, many mobile customers are accustomed to receiving text messages riddled with abbreviations from friends, while those using the BlackBerry's built-in BlackBerry Messenger service have no length limitations to begin with.

Most cell phones sold by major phone companies in the United States today come preloaded with MMS capability, meaning thousands of different types of phones can receive video. Mobile phone companies typically view SMS and MMS as identical for customer billing purposes.

If the majority of your customers are using smartphones already, you have more options in your mobile marketing arsenal, though SMS and MMS may still be a worthwhile part of your marketing mix. More than half of those with smartphones already regularly send pictures or video,[98] showing that many customers are already comfortable dealing with different media types in addition to text. Another advantage of many smartphones is the size and quality of the screen, which offers a better experience for images and video. But if your customers have a wide variety of phones, your probability of being able to reach them with SMS or MMS is very high, because nearly all mobile phones in use today have the capacity to receive these messages.

The advantage of MMS is that you can send a text message but can include an image or video to enhance it. In some cases, MMS is almost a necessity because of the length of text required. A pharmaceutical company, for example, is legally required to include lengthy disclosure information with its marketing messages, which would not fit within a standard SMS message.

A significant number of phones (in the hundreds of millions globally) are video enabled, a number that will only increase as older handsets are replaced. As mobile video consumption rises, untethered consumers will come to expect that some of the marketing messages they receive will be in video format. Expectations for more interesting and more sophisticated mobile messages will continue to rise with the growing technical capacities of the phones.

Mobile Results with MMS

The leading pioneer in MMS marketing is Mogreet. The company was founded in 2006 in Venice, California, by James Citron, and focused almost exclusively on mobile video marketing. The company facilitates the delivery of mobile video by MMS and has served clients including Reebok, Warner Brothers, Starwood Hotels, Steve Madden, Nike, and American Greetings.

The company set out to take text messaging to the next level, by including video: "We talked about a lot of ideas and ultimately wanted to create something better than text," says Citron, who is Chief Executive Officer.[99] "The carriers and handset manufacturers got together and created an MMS standard because the market needed something better than SMS." Just as others had in different segments of the mobile industry, Mogreet created a platform for marketers to use and named it the Mogreet Messaging System. Like many of the other platforms discussed in this book, the Mogreet video mobile marketing platform provides self-service operations for businesses together with detailed reporting and analysis of results.

Unlike the early days of the Internet, when measurements of success included how many people looked at a Web page, mobile and MMS hold greater promise of precise measurements of effectiveness and success. There are several reasons for this:

- Mobile is personal. It is known that a message was delivered to a specific person.
- By opting in, the customer agrees in advance to accept your marketing messages. You start with a more receptive customer.
- You can measure results of a call to action, so you can see exactly how many customers entered a contest, claimed a coupon, or bought a product.
- You can tell where and when an action occurred. With the Web you could measure the *when* but not the *where*. Mobile changes that. It can show you where your messages are most effective.

Mogreet is part of the mobile revolution that many people don't see. The company's video platform reaches more than 200 million mobile phones in the United States and uses all the major cell phone carriers. But, like many other companies in the mobile industry, Mogreet sells its services to other companies to use, on a business-to-business, or B-to-B, basis.

As a consumer, you may have seen a video provided by a company using the Mogreet platform, though you would not realize it because the video comes from a brand you know and there is nothing in it that emphasizes the platform itself. If you're a marketer or agency that specializes in mobile, still a relatively small club, you likely know of the MMS platform.

As mobile multimedia increases, mobile platforms such as those from Mogreet will comprise the underlying foundation that companies will use to interact with their customers. These platforms will act as the mobile customer relationship management (CRM) system for companies.

Mobile facilitates messaging. Though the mobile industry started with voice communication, text has grown exponentially because senders and receivers can do it asynchronously, each on their own timeframe. Enormous growth in MMS was the expectation when Mogreet started. Says Citron:

> When we started the company we saw that mobile messaging was the way the world was going to communicate. We started with the premise that over time the preferred way to receive mobile messages was going to be by rich media.
>
> We started with looking at what do customers and businesses want and how were they communicating. Consumers were sending and receiving pictures and videos, since MMS started as peer to peer consumer.
>
> And then we saw that ten billion mobile greeting cards were sent in 2005 for Chinese New Year throughout China, and that was just person to person. That was a turning point for us. We figured if you can create a platform to facilitate the sending of cards of one to many that would be big. And we also thought that for phones the only way accomplish this was MMS.
>
> But MMS is very hard. Every piece of content has to be formatted and optimized for each device and carrier. We add twenty to thirty new mobile devices a week to add a system that can deliver MMS content to more than seven thousand different mobile devices from the Motorola RAZRs to iPhones to iPads. The system has to detect the characteristics of each device to deliver a MMS to the phone. The good news is that the Mogreet MMS platform can detect what kind of phone it is and if it can receive a video.

Billions of messages are sent over the Mogreet platform by companies of all sizes and in all categories. Citron says that opening and viewing rates of the MMS messages are typically 15 to 25 percent higher than they are with other advertising media, and the MMS messages are nearly 20 percent more effective than standard text messages. And because the videos are often shared among friends, the total audience for a marketer's MMS message can increase significantly. Following are some examples of companies that have used the Mogreet platform:

Reebok. The company wanted to build a database of mobile consumers to whom it could promote a new line of apparel, so it invited consumers to watch a mobile video and enter a sweepstakes. The mobile video featured various NFL athletes, and the company promoted it on various social media websites focused on young athletes and football fans. Consumers were asked to text REEBOK to a short code number, and they received a return message inviting them to opt in. If the consumer's phone supported video, the Mogreet platform automatically sent the video via MMS and if it did not, the platform sent a link to a website where the consumer could view it from a computer. Approximately 50 percent of those who received the message clicked to open the offer.

Hotel Casa del Mar. This Santa Monica, California, hotel saw the advantage of building a list of opted-in mobile customers, so it created a special offer for guests that encouraged them to join the hotel's loyalty club. The hotel added the MMS text message information to its hotel marketing materials and on cash register receipts. By texting CASA to a short code number provided, consumers received a mobile video they could use to redeem an unlimited number of certain drinks free at the hotel during Sunday brunch. The campaign showed that 72 percent of the messages were sent to mobile phones in the Los Angeles metropolitan area, the hotel's target customer location. The campaign had a delivery rate of 100 percent, an engagement rate of 75 percent, a 27 percent redemption rate, and a significant number of people added to the hotel's mobile database.

American Greetings. The greeting cards company decided to allow customers to send video cards selected from its website directly to recipients' phones, to extend the reach of its marketing to mobile consumers. The customer inputs the mobile phone number at the e-card section of the American Greetings website, selects a greeting, and sends a card that includes full-motion sounds and video, for a fee. During Valentine's Day, consumers in every state in the United States sent and received greeting cards across thirty different cell phone carriers and more than a thousand mobile phone types.

Nike and the NFL. This partnership created a mobile video campaign for the 2010 Super Bowl. Fifteen percent of those who opted in to the program and received exclusive NFL content via MMS shared that content with someone else, demonstrating the significant viral sharing opportunities available through MMS.

Steve Madden is using MMS for Fashion Look books, featuring video of celebrities wearing Steve Madden shoes, as well as enabling consumers to receive pictures and videos of their favorite shoes and music videos from their favorite Madden Music artists.

Various additional market segments also have begun using MMS in some of their marketing campaigns, including movie studios. "Dozens of top movies, including ten number-ones at the box office, have been marketed via our MMS platform," says Citron. "These include *Twilight, 17 Again, Slumdog Millionaire, Charlie St. Cloud*, and *The Kids Are Alright.*" Fitness companies, too, are seeing the possibilities for marketing with MMS. The national children's fitness chain MyGym sends bimonthly fitness tips to the mobile phones of parents to help encourage exercise and combat childhood obesity, while reinforcing its brand.

Companies are using Mogreet's MMS platform to communicate not only with customers, but also internally. Sales departments in some Fortune 1000 companies also use the platform for sales force communications; for example the vice president of sales can send to the team various sales announcements, motivational speeches, promotions, and education and training materials.

The Pull of the Consumer

With SMS and MMS, marketers connect with customers by offering value and asking customers if they want to opt in to various programs. There are times, however, when a business provides such high inherent value that those incentives are not needed. Instead, customers pull the information to them without being asked.

Among the most commonly sought pieces of information on mobile (and on the web, for that matter) are weather conditions and forecasts. After all, weather affects almost everyone. Is it going to rain this afternoon? Will it be warm tomorrow? Is snow coming? And when people want to know about the weather, they want to know now. The weather impacts our lives: what we wear, what we do, where we go. And when it comes to providing that sought-after content, people turn to The Weather Channel, owners of weather.com, which is ranked the twentieth-largest website in the world. Consider these stats about The Weather Channel:

- More than twenty-two million people a month access the weather via its mobile app.
- More than 1.2 billion pages a month are seen from the mobile app (online it is 1.1 billion).
- More than fifty million MMS messages per month are viewed on phones.

While some may attribute the success of The Weather Channel on mobile to owning the name "weather," as in weather.com, the reality is that the company spent more than a decade developing, structuring, building, and growing its mobile presence. "In 1999, we launched our first mobile site and it started growing," says Cameron Clayton, Senior Vice President of Mobile and Digital Applications at The Weather Channel.[100] "In 2002 we launched our first Java app, downloaded with AT&T. The application took off. In 2004 and 2005 we got into the SMS/MMS business."

Clayton, who has been with The Weather Channel for half a dozen years, worked in business development before taking over the mobile team a few years ago. The group is staffed by more than fifty people, including about two dozen in the technology department, which may seem like a lot to some. However, the business has the rather rare requirement of delivering round-the-clock, up-do-date weather content to mobile consumers on multiple devices everywhere, increasingly via mobile apps.

There was a turning point where the management team at The Weather Channel decided to invest in mobile. Says Clayton:

> From 1999 until 2007, mobile at The Weather Channel was growing, but it didn't start out as strategic. We were experimenting and testing

with what worked best for the consumer and for our business. Then in 2007, the iPhone came out and changed everything. This was not just a change in devices, but a change in human behavior. It made people's lives easier. It was—and still is—a global phenomenon. In 2007, we estimated that there would be about 1.6 billion cell phones in a few years' time, but in reality there are now four and a half billion cell phones out of six billion people on the planet. The mobile effect impacts everyone. For example, in some parts of the world, like areas of rural India, there are illiterate people who can't read a newspaper but can recognize the design of key characters, so they are sending text messages to communicate.

At this worldwide turning point in 2007, The Weather Channel was already established on mobile, so we realized we were part of a behavioral change in the global population. We decided to invest early, bringing all our mobile development in-house. Our approach was to be early to market in order to establish our leadership role and to try and lead in the smartphone space.

For us it started as a subscription-based revenue story, starting with paid subscriptions at $2.99 a month. However, the market's transition to an ad-supported, free-to-consumer model has really come to fruition in the last nine months. The doubt for mobile has always been how quickly we can use ads to monetize the business, but now advertising revenue doubles that of subscriptions. At The Weather Channel, we had always hoped and planned for the transition to an ad-supported model because that's our core business. We know the digital advertising business—weather.com is our sweet spot, and now we are a leader in the mobile advertising space as well.

Mobile is evolving rapidly, but mobile is now strategic for us. The growth of mobile has not only transformed how our organization builds apps but also how we interact with the consumer. Customers first viewed TWC as a television property, then they accepted a more interactive TWC online at weather.com, and now they are increasingly finding us on mobile, where they can take the weather with them wherever they go. Now, in 2010, TWC is the leading cross-platform media company—consumers use TWC the most across all platforms, including television, online, and mobile. The growth and maturation of media and its consumption has a broad impact, and mobile is in the middle of that evolution. The mobile device is a very intimate and personal item. It is your life that you carry with you. We think of the important three things—wallet, keys, and cell phone. If you leave your phone at home, you'll turn around for it because it's the ultimate communication device. It's also a very personalized way to reach your users. We are a strong cross-platform brand, but mobile is different. TV delivers one piece of content to a broad audience—the reach is one-to-many—while PC offers a one-to-less reach. However, mobile allows us a one-to-one reach, fully tailoring the content for that user.

Clayton does not see other weather providers as the main competitors for The Weather Channel on mobile. "We're competing for consumers' time," he says. "We have 80 percent of market share in the weather category, but we look to grow that market share in other categories. Social media and portals are our competitors in terms of the number of minutes."

Says Clayton:

Consumers who invest a lot of time in our platform are more loyal, and the likelihood that they will switch is low. One of the opportunities we are working on is to involve our customers in a user-generated, participatory service, such has having them give us the weather. Weather has been presented the same way for thirty years, but it needs to adapt to technology and to the consumer. The Weather Channel can lead that redefinition with the help of our mobile users—the ones who are actually out in the weather with their mobile devices. We will encourage our users to participate and be engaged so we can use a shared, crowd-sourcing model to improve our forecasts. They can report weather to each other and even rate the weather, engage with fantasy forecasters, or even compete against us—all ways to get personally invested in us.

In addition to more social, user-generated content, we are also focused on growing internationally. For now, the company has international websites in seven countries and mobile content in seven languages. The Weather Channel continues to look for other areas for growth as well to keep our leadership position. Our plan has served us well, resulting in numerous top rankings. Weather is one of the most requested categories on mobile, and we are consistently ranked as the top mobile weather content provider. We're the cross-platform usage leader among media companies, the number-one content provider on mobile web, the top weather app on all smartphones, and the number-two most popular app overall on all smartphones, according to Nielsen. We were named the top iPhone app of 2009, and the fact that Apple featured The Weather Channel app in a TV spot told us something. Happy consumers return to those mobile resources that provide them what they need when they need it.

Strategy, Goals, and Flexibility

Like many companies, The Weather Channel may focus on smartphone capabilities, but not at the peril of other opportunities. "We want to be where people are, and there are 140 million feature phones," says The Weather Channel's Cameron Clayton. "We develop for eight hundred different mobile phones even though our focus is on smartphones."

However, by riding the smartphone wave, The Weather Channel has also been able to capitalize on providing opportunities for other marketers who want to reach their customers through their smartphones. "The idea is to be able to offer a hot latte when a person is in the area of a local Dunkin' Donuts and the weather conditions call for a warm drink, or to have the opportunity to purchase a train ticket for the Amtrak Acela no matter where you stand along the Eastern Corridor," says Pete Chelala, Mobile Specialist at The Weather Channel.[101] "Since the Acela consumer is a business traveler and uses his mobile devices for instant access and convenience, it makes sense to reach him via the mobile platform."

Like many of the large mobile content sites, The Weather Channel markets advertising opportunities for its mobile weather content and has witnessed the growth of capabilities offered by smartphones. "We're starting to get RFPs [Requests for Proposals] strictly on mobile budgets," says Chelala. He sees plans to use the geotargeting capabilities of smartphones to increase the relevance of marketing messages based on time and location.

While your business may not have as significant a mobile presence as The Weather Channel, there are still many mobile opportunities likely to present themselves once you're in the game. The Weather Channel had a distinct advantage with its early entry into the mobile marketplace; the company had already created a mobile platform by the time the iPhone was introduced, making it easier to identify a significant market shift. And while the revenue model was at first subscriptions-based, bringing in double the advertising revenue, market dynamics shifted that model to exactly the opposite almost overnight. The key in mobile marketing is to have a strategy, goals, and above all else, flexibility.

CHAPTER 10

The New Laws of (Inbound) Mobile Marketing

Where mobile goes from here and how we, as marketers keep up, are core questions. The technology will continue to improve, with increasing processing speeds, faster networks, and more innovations in applications and features coming out of the mobile industry. Smartphone adoption will continue to increase as well.

More significant, the behaviors of untethered consumers will continue to evolve and fundamentally alter how companies and brands interact with them. Businesses will have to rethink how they market and communicate to these consumers. Messaging in a world gone mobile needs to be short, relevant, and effective. And those interactions have to provide constant value to the mobile customer.

Companies will have to move marketing from an inside-out approach to one that is permission-based and outside-in. This means that rather than companies sending marketing or advertising messages from inside the company outside to the individual, it will be the untethered consumer who is requesting the information or service from the outside. With mobile, the m-powered customer is in charge. Making this transition will be challenging for many, as a long, drawn-out marketing campaign can totally miss the market of the on-the-go, untethered consumer. That consumer will be contacting the company when something is desired, on the consumer's timeframe and based on their location.

The third screen is already redefining the way consumers absorb messaging and changing the way they interact with the brands they value. These m-powered customers are watching video from their phones, they're shopping, and they're buying. Their appetite for useful information based on location will only increase as they see the benefit that others obtain from using mobile services.

The third screen revolution provides companies with a great opportunity to interact with customers on a more intimate level, because the smartphone is so personal and kept close to the user. The untethered consumer will demand value from this connection; companies will need to create incentives for consumers to connect with them, providing a win–win for both parties. And the third screen will forever transform the concept of one to-one marketing, allowing a company to market directly to the untethered consumer as he shops.

Mobile provides vast opportunities for traditional brick-and-mortar retailers, as customers shopping in their stores access real-time information about their products. Brands of all sizes have been anxiously awaiting this development, which will give them the opportunity to conduct what I call *momentary marketing*. This allows companies to market to the customer at precisely the time and location that is of most value to both the customer and the company, the moment of the purchase decision.

These moments will come and go, as the customer moves from location to location, always armed with her mobile information source.

Mobile Innovation

The nascent mobile industry will continue to evolve. It has already produced mobile platforms, innovative ways to transmit mobile video, services that leverage phone locations, and services that allow customers to interact in multiple ways. It has devised ways to enable a customer to scan a product and ways that companies can create additional digital value associated with that product.

Mobile payment systems will also evolve, as customers have already proven themselves comfortable with making mobile purchases, even if only from apps stores. Companies will figure out how to construct new models of mobile that incorporate on-the-go, pay-from-your-phone features. One innovative marketing company in Belgium, for example, has been experimenting with giving consumers product samples. The agency, Fosfor, created a stand-alone machine called the Boobox that distributes samples of soft drinks. Consumers use their cell phones to text a message to the company, and they receive an activation code by SMS message. Then they use the code at the machine to receive a free sample. The idea of sending text messages to a company and receiving codes in return could evolve to sending payment authorization. Mobile devices will be used to control DVRs and TVs, unlock doors, and start cars.

There will be mobile experimentation, just as there is in other areas of marketing. This process will be much like the retail practice of placing impulse items along the checkout lanes. While retailers can't yet precisely identify the impulse buyer, they have learned over time which products tend to sell best, and hence are defined as impulse items. The result is essentially the same as it would be if the retailers could identify the impulse buyers: the impulse items sell. There will be similar mobile experiments, although with mobile, tracking results can be far more precise, removing some of the guesswork.

Do Something

Mobile customers, by definition, can be reached wherever they are, and their phones are always on. Never before could both the right location and the right time be factored into marketing, but with new mobile technologies, companies can know when their customers are primed to act. Those businesses willing to take a test-and-learn approach, to find out how their customers want to interact with them, can feel comfortable that they are less likely to be left behind.

But for the test-and-learn approach of mobile marketing to succeed, you need to start. As simple as that sounds, many businesses are waiting and watching what others are doing. The problem with that approach (or lack of approach) is that you don't learn what does and doesn't work in mobile with your customers.

"We're finding clients are starting to understand a little bit," says Hugh Jedwill, CEO of Mobile Anthem, a mobile-only advertising agency based in Chicago.[102] "Some are intrigued by it but are saying, 'You haven't convinced me yet.' We have to show how it will help move their key business metrics." Jedwill, who has worked on mobile campaigns with Procter & Gamble, Sara Lee, and candy manufacturer JustBorn, sees challenges within certain parts of organizations when it comes to mobile marketing. "Not everyone in the room gets it," he says. "The younger people get it but some of those older do not. We give them insights into their consumers as it relates to mobile. They know mobile is big, we just have to show them how it has changed their consumers' behaviors."

Mobile Anthem has conducted mobile campaigns in which a client company provided samples to people who were reached via their mobile phones, allowing better customer targeting and easier response by untethered consumers. For example, in a mobile campaign for a Sara Lee product, Mobile Anthem launched a game where customers could text for a chance to win. The intent was to drive customers back to a store, so the company sent another text message detailing all the additional prizes available. Thousands of customers texted messages over the two-week period of the promotion, and Mobile Anthem found that people continually checked the mobile website each time a text message was sent.

"Traffic continued to grow on the mobile website," says Jedwill. "We were changing behavior. Not only can you drive behavior with mobile, you can also drive habits. But don't forget you still have to manage people's expectations so they understand upfront how often you will message them. Sometimes the best path for mobile is to just do something. You should include mobile in wherever you can, but make sure you're dealing with someone who knows mobile, not just the digital guy at your agency who was just assigned mobile last month. It should be in a test-and-learn type of situation."

There are relatively simple ways to test mobile marketing to start your own learning process, if it's not under way already. These range from adding a mobile component, such as a text message campaign like the Sara Lee launched, to the research-based approach of Procter & Gamble through Vocalpoint, discussed earlier in the book.

Marketers cannot expand their brands' reach in a world gone mobile without some experience, which can only be gotten by actually doing something and analyzing the results.

Mobile Verb Branding

It's common knowledge that Google is the king of Web search. A clear indicator that a company has reached "king" position is when it achieves what we call "verb branding"[103] status. When you FedEx a package, the implication is that the package can be traced every step of the way, will be handled properly, and will be delivered to its intended destination precisely when promised. When you Amazon a book or DVD, it is expected that the entire transaction will be easy, the billing will be accurate, the product will be sent and delivered when promised, and if there are any problems, Amazon customer service will resolve them quickly and easily. When someone says "Facebook me," she wants you to connect with her and send a message via Facebook. These are all cases of verb branding, where the overall experience that offers value to the customer becomes the actual product, rather than the nominal product or service. The company creates a platform so powerful that the activity of doing its thing supersedes the identity of the products themselves.

Thinking about what a brand would represent as a verb can help stimulate thinking about the business the company is actually in. This is a chance for a business to explore what true value they represent to their customers. Google achieved verb-branding status; when you "Google" something, you expect that the most relevant search results will be presented to you almost instantaneously. Yes, you can *use* Bing or Yahoo, but rather than *use* Google, you "Google" something.

As mobile matures as an industry, verb-branded companies, products, and applications will emerge. One early example came via Research in Motion's BlackBerry messaging services. BlackBerry users "BBM" each other. Verb branding cannot be simply decided and promoted, it has to be earned. Mobile, more than any other platform, lends itself to creation of verb-branded products and services.

Bumps Along the Way

Like all technological–behavioral transformations before it, the third screen revolution will not progress without bumps, obstacles, and detours along the way. Just as personal computer operating systems improved over time, so too will the underlying technologies and capabilities of smartphones. As anyone with a smartphone knows, there are still issues with connectivity and availability in some locations.

In a world gone mobile, customers will become increasingly aware of how much information can be automatically sent from their phones. Over time, they will decide what they want to share and with whom they want to share it. Some customers may not want others to know their location, at any time, so they may opt out of that feature on their smartphone, and they need to be assured of that right. Companies need to confirm that their customers opt in before interacting with them in any meaningful way, and they need to make it very easy for customers to opt out, for whatever reason, at any time. Businesses risk betraying customers' trust by sharing their information inappropriately, and those businesses that do will pay dearly with reputation.

Another challenge that both customers and marketers will have to deal with is mobile information overload. Because customers' phones can be pinpointed, if they so choose, they risk receiving an onslaught of information from multiple sources as they traverse through their daily routines. Customers will determine which platforms they use, ranging from mobile social networking platforms to those provided by individual companies and brands or aggregators.

There is the issue of apps overload as well. With hundreds of thousands of apps available for smartphones, and with the number growing daily, customers may not know where to find the most effective apps for them. Conversely, they may download so many apps that they end up not using any because their screens are too cluttered.

It's Not About the Phone, It's About the Value

Perhaps the most significant hurdle for mobile will be achieving the large-scale adoption of the new capabilities by those who have not yet moved to smartphones. These consumers may be technologically challenged, budget restrained, or resistant to changes in the way they interact, shop, or behave.

However, as more people see the value of smartphone features demonstrated by other mobile users, they may want to achieve similar results. When they see other shoppers scanning items and getting on-the-spot discounts, they can become instant converts. It's not about the phone, it's about the value. Marketers cannot afford to wait until all of their customers adopt mobile, or they will have a hard time catching up. Consumers are already moving ahead at great speed. They are driving the market.

And mobile is the ultimate measurement vehicle, because a message can be tied directly to customer action. If a customer clicked or tapped a commercial message, the marketer can determine at what location and what time that action occurred.

But it still comes down to the value the company is providing its customers through their phones. Knowing when those customers are active and where those customers are going gives businesses a totally new opportunity to match time, distance, supply, and demand, since each of those is now measurable. Those who do this win.

Companies must recognize that the mobile revolution is more than just an additional sales channel or one more place to advertise. It involves fundamental changes in consumer behavior at all levels, and it changes and heightens expectations of customers.

The ultimate impact of this global phenomenon called mobile will be bigger than the impact of television or the personal computer. It is everywhere, it is personal, and it is always on. Welcome to the world of the third screen.

ENDNOTES

1. List of more than 1,000 mobile companies funded in the course of the research for the book supplied to author.
2. World population estimate of 6,864,071,404 from the U.S. Census Bureau.
3. Based on data from The European Information Technology Observatory, also known as EITO.
4. Cell phone usages estimate from CTIA: The Wireless Association and U.S. population data from the U.S. Census Bureau.
5. Data from the International Telecommunication Union, also known as ITU.
6. Data from the International Telecommunication Union, also known as ITU.
7. Based on research from the Nielsen Company.
8. Based on CTIA Wireless' semiannual wireless industry survey results.
9. Based on research from comScore.
10. Based on the author's interview with Michael Becker, North American Managing Director, Mobile Market Association.
11. From comments made by Thomas Knoll, Community Architect at Zappos, at MediaPost's Mobile Insider Summit and in discussions with the author.
12. Based on research from the Knowledge Networks KnowledgePanel, a research panel representative of the U.S. population as a whole.
13. Based on research provided to the author by InsightExpress.
14. Following research provided to the author by InsightExpress.
15. Based on research provided to the author by InsightExpress.
16. Based on research provided to the author by Knowledge Networks.
17. Based on research provided to the author by InsightExpress.

18. The owners of Classified Ventures include five major media companies: Belo Corp., Gannett Co., The McClatchy Co., Tribune Co., and The Washington Post Co.
19. Based on the author's interview with Nick Fotis, Products Manager, Mobile, at Cars.com
20. Data from the ITU World Telecommunication.
21. Research from the Nielsen Company.
22. Research from the Nielsen Company.
23. This and the following two examples were created by Mobext, a mobile marketing agency that is part of the Havas Digital group of agencies.
24. The program was created by Hotmob Ltd., the largest mobile advertising media network in Hong Kong with technology partner GreenTomato.
25. Based on the author's interview with Leisa Glispy, Group Director of Global e-Commerce, Waterford Wedgwood Royal Doulton.
26. The following industry data is from CTIA: The Wireless Association and Motorola.
27. Based on data and projections from The Nielsen Company.
28. Based on research provided to the author by InsightExpress.
29. This and the immediately following data points from the InsightExpress study provided to the author.
30. Concept from decision process by Chase Martin while determining next smartphone to acquire.
31. Comments from Cheryl Lucanegro, Senior Vice President, Pandora, at MediaPost's Mobile Insider Summit, and recorded by the author.
32. Based on the Mobile Consumer Research report provided to the author by InsightExpress.
33. Phone sales data from global research firm IDC.
34. Based on research from AdMob Mobile Metrics, a Google-owned company that serves ads for more than 23,000 mobile Web sites and applications globally.
35. Operating system estimates from Gartner, Inc., a global information technology research and advisory company.
36. Based on the author's interview with Greg Johnson, Director of Digital Ventures, Playboy.
37. Based on research provided to the author by Knowledge Networks.
38. Based on research provided to the author by Knowledge Networks.
39. Based on research provided to the author by Knowledge Networks.
40. Based on the author's interview with Nagraj Kashyap, Vice President, Qualcomm Ventures.
41. Based on the author's interview with Jack Young, Senior Investment Manager, Qualcomm Ventures.

42. Based on one month viewership in Nielsen's 2010 Three Screens Report.
43. Based on VideoCensus data from The Nielsen Company.
44. The following is based on the author's interview with Marc Theermann, Vice President of Mobile at AdMeld.
45. Based on the author's interview with Paul Kultgen, Director of Mobile Media and Advertising, The Nielsen Company.
46. Based on the author's interview with Andrew Koven, President of e-Commerce and Customer Experience, Steve Madden Ltd.
47. Based on a survey by the Mobile Future Institute.
48. Based on the official PepsiCo World Headquarters materials describing the complex.
49. Based on the author's interview with B. Bonin Bough, Director of Digital and Social Media, PepsiCo.
50. Based on the author's interview with John Vail, Director of Interactive Marketing Group, Pepsi Cola Beverages.
51. Comments by Shiv Singh, Director of Digital, North America, PepsiCo, as recorded by the author at the MediaPost Change: Digital Transformation Summit in Boston.
52. Based on the author's interview with Matthew Roth of Intel.
53. Based on the author's interview with Lucas Frank, Brand Manager, Jeep.
54. Based on the author's interview with Stephen Surman, Relationship Marketing Manager, Vocalpoint, a division of Procter & Gamble.
55. From comments made by Howard Hunt, Vice President of New Business Development, The Hyperfactory, at the MediaPost Mobile Insider Summit, and recorded by the author.
56. Based on the author's interview with Peter Velikin, Vice President of Marketing, Zmags.
57. Based on the author's interview with Josh Koppel, cofounder of ScrollMotion.
58. Based on the author's interview with Yaron Galai, founder and CEO, Outbrain.
59. Data on Internet video viewership from comScore for May 2010.
60. This and the following research provided to the author by InsightExpress.
61. Based on research provided to the author by Knowledge Networks.
62. Based on research provided to the author by Knowledge Networks.
63. Based on the author's interview with Gannon Hall, Chief Operating Officer, Kyte.

64. Quote attributed to Philadelphia merchant John Wanamaker(1838–1922), who is widely credited as the father of modern advertising.

65. Based on the author's interview with Boris Fridman, Chief Executive Officer, Crisp Wireless.

66. Based on the official announcement by Spot Inc.

67. Based on the author's interview with JJ Beh, Mortgage Strategy and Planning Lead, ING Direct.

68. Based on the author's interview with Phuc Truong, Managing Director, U.S. Mobile Mobile Marketing, Mobext.

69. Results based only on the respondents who were on the panel; not projectable across the population.

70. This and the following data are based on data from research firm NCH Marketing Services, Inc.

71. Based on mid-year 2010 data from research firm NCH Marketing Services, Inc.

72. Data reported was for a twelve-month period ended June 30, 2010.

73. Based on data from research firm NCH Marketing Services, Inc.

74. Based on research provided to the author by InsightExpress.

75. Data from "Mobile Marketing Study: Expectations, Realities, and Payback," conducted by The Center for Media Research, MediaPost Communications, with InsightExpress.

76. Based on the author's interview with Steve Horowitz, Chief Technology Officer, Coupons.com.

77. Demonstrated live by Horowitz for the author and later live at the MediaPost Mobile Insider Summit at Lake Tahoe.

78. Based on the author's interview with Brian Wilson, cofounder and Vice President of Marketing, Point Inside.

79. Based on the author's interview with Ankit Agarwal, founder and CEO, Micello.

80. Based on the author's interview with Ted Murphy, founder and CEO, IZEA, the company that launched WeReward.

81. Based on the author's interview with Alistair Goodman, Chief Executive Officer, Placecast (officially 1020, Inc.)

82. The program is named after its creator, Stephen Wolfram, who in 2009 launched the long-term project in an attempt to make as much of the world's knowledge as possible computable and accessible to everyone.

83. Based on the author's interview with Steve Larsen, cofounder, PhoneTell.

84. From the Wrigley heritage timeline.

85. Based on comments from Dudley Fitzpatrick, founder, Jagtag, made at MediaPost's Mobile Insider Summit and recorded by the author.

86. Based on the author's interview with Jane McPherson, Chief Marketing Officer of SpyderLink.
87. Based on the author's interview with David Javitch, Vice President Marketing, Scanbuy.
88. Based on comments by David Plant, Director of Mobile, PGA Tour, at MediaPost's Mobile Insider Summit and recorded by the author.
89. Statistics on usage from Facebook.
90. Based on research provided to the author by InsightExpress.
91. This and the following data based on research provided to the author by InsightExpress.
92. Based on the author's interview with Eric Friedman, Director of Client Services, Foursquare.
93. Based on the author's interview with BJ Emerson, Social Technology Officer, Tasti D-Lite.
94. Based on annual studies conducted by CTIA—The Wireless Association.
95. Based on estimates from ABI Research from its Mobile Messaging Services study at the end of 2010.
96. Opt-in and opt-out guidelines are issued by the Mobile Marketing Association.
97. Based on the author's interview with Jared Reitzin, CEO and Chairman, mobileStorm
98. Based on research provided to the author by Knowledge Networks.
99. Based on the author's interview with James Citron, CEO and cofounder, Mogreet.
100. Based on the author's interview with Cameron Clayton, Senior Vice President of Mobile and Digital Applications, The Weather Channel.
101. Based on the author's interview with Pete Chelala, Mobile Specialist, The Weather Channel.
102. Based on the author's interview with Hugh Jedwill, CEO, Mobile Anthem.
103. The term "verb branding" was coined by the author in *Max-e-Marketing in the Net Future* (McGraw-Hill, 2001), coauthored with Stan Rapp.

ABOUT THE AUTHOR

Chuck Martin has been a leading pioneer in the digital interactive marketplace for more than a decade. He was early and accurate in predicting the Web revolution, and is now forecasting a new revolution, this time in mobile.

Martin is CEO and founder of The Mobile Future Institute and Director of the Center for Media Research at MediaPost Communications. As a digital pioneer, researcher, and public speaker, he has his thumb on the pulse of the mobile marketplace.

In his newest book, *The Third Screen*, Martin defines the implications, strategies, and tactics for businesses to thrive in this coming mobile revolution. This book links the technological developments to the behavioral changes that go hand-in-hand and reveals the unexpected aspects of the coming changes in mobile, preparing marketers and businesspeople for what is looming in the near future.

The Mobile Future Institute is a U.S-based think tank that focuses on business strategies and marketing tactics for a world gone mobile—delving into how, when, and where marketers should best interact with mobile customers. The Institute and Martin are in the forefront of mobile research, exploring how the untethered consumer is on the move, on location, and how marketers can most effectively reach them in this new digital landscape.

At the Center for Media Research at MediaPost Communications, Martin conducts and markets original research for media, marketing, and advertising professionals. The Center provides a dependable source of insight to help media professionals identify trends and patterns in traditional and online advertising. Martin also is the brand manager for MediaPost's Mobile Insider Summits, held in Lake Tahoe and Florida.

Martin is a former Vice President of IBM, where he ran a division responsible for business strategy solutions in the media industry, including publishers and advertising agencies. He is a *New York Times* business bestselling author of numerous books, including *The Digital Estate*, *Net Future*, and *Max-e-Marketing in the Net Future* (co-author). Martin was the founding Publisher of *Interactive Age,* the first publication to launch in print and on the Web simultaneously, and was Associate Publisher at *Information Week*, a magazine targeted to CIOs and information technology professionals. Martin has been Editor-in-Chief of four national magazines and a journalist at five daily newspapers.

He is a highly sought-after speaker, represented by the leading speakers' bureaus. He is the former host of a daily business technology show and he has appeared on CNN, CNBC, Fox Business, ABC-TV News Now, and regularly appears on TV and numerous radio shows across the country.

About The Mobile Future Institute

The Mobile Future Institute is a U.S.-based think tank focused on business strategies and marketing tactics for a world gone mobile. The organization explores how the mobile consumer is on the move, on location, and how marketers will have to find and interact with their customers where they are in this new digital landscape.

The Mobile Future Institute delves into the mobile marketplace to determine how, when, and where marketers should best interact with mobile customers, beyond coupons and discounts. The institute is led by *New York Times* business bestselling author Chuck Martin, who has been a leading pioneer in the digital interactive marketplace for more than a decade. Martin is a noted researcher and is also Director of the Center of Media Research at MediaPost Communications.

The Institute regularly surveys more than one thousand business leaders around the world. Some of those survey results are included in this book. The surveys are short and results are anonymous. These surveys have been conducted regularly for the past ten years.

When the questions list potential answers, the Institute asks respondents in the panel to check all answers that apply, thereby providing a majority consensus in results. The surveys do not necessarily match intensity of feeling about any given subject, but rather what the majority of respondents agree and disagree on. The Institute does not share e-mail addresses or any personal information about any of its members. There is no charge for membership, and the members all receive the survey results for free. Response rates are typically at least 10 percent. The survey results are routinely reported in newspapers, magazines, newsletters, and blogs around the world.

Survey participants fall into one of two categories: senior executive (chief executive officer, chairman, president, chief operating officer, chief financial officer, chief information officer, executive vice president, senior vice president, general manager, etc.) or manager (assistant vice president, director, manager, supervisor, etc.). Respondents are usually about half senior executives and half managers. Some percentages do not equal 100 percent due to rounding. All research in the book, unless otherwise stated, is primary research conducted by Chuck Martin or The Mobile Future Institute.

Respondents also identify themselves by company size, based on total number of employees, and the results generally are a fairly even split among the groups. Company sizes are based on number of employees, with small having 1 to 499 employees, medium 500 to 9999, and large with 10,000 or more employees.

A small sampling of the more than one thousand companies for which members work are IBM, GE, Morgan Stanley, Microsoft, CIGNA, Fidelity, Merck, Motorola, Freddie Mac, Progressive, Travelers, MasterCard, Sears Roebuck, SAP, Oracle, Sony, Marriott International, Mercer, American Gas, Heineken, Western Energy Institute, WalMart, Wells Fargo, ABN AMRO Bank, Air Canada, Agilent Technologies, Allied Waste Industries, American Association of Advertising Agencies, American Cancer Society, American Express, Apple, 3M Company, AT&T, Bank of America, Bell Canada, Bell South, Best Buy, California Credit Union League, Bristol-Meyers Squibb Company, Canon, Delta Air Lines, Unilever, and Procter and Gamble.

You may obtain further information at *www.MobileFutureInstitute. com*, where you may apply for free membership. You may also contact the author directly at *Chuck@MobileFutureInstitute.com* and follow him on Twitter at *www.twitter.com/chuckmartin1*, or @chuckmartin1.

INDEX